BR
115
.C8
S6

Sockman
Date with destiny

D0004757

Date Due

Date With Destiny, A Preamble To Christi
BR115.C8S6   3633

Sockman, Ralph Washington
VRJC/WRIGHT LIBRARY

BRO
DART   PRINTED IN U.S.A.

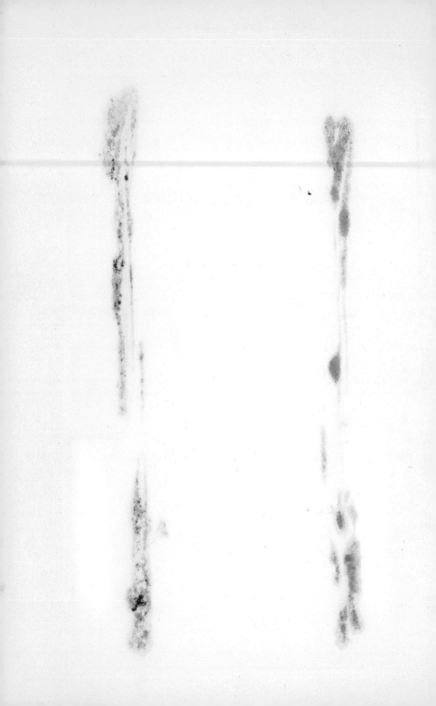

DATE WITH DESTINY

BOOKS BY RALPH W. SOCKMAN

THE WHOLE ARMOR OF GOD
DATE WITH DESTINY
THE HIGHER HAPPINESS
NOW TO LIVE!

DATE WITH DESTINY

A Preamble to Christian Culture *by* RALPH W. SOCKMAN *THE* FONDREN LECTURES FOR 1943

NEW YORK *Abingdon Press* NASHVILLE

REGIONAL JUNIOR COLLEGE LIBRARY

DATE WITH DESTINY

Copyright MCMXLIV by Whitmore & Stone

All rights in this book are reserved.
No part of the book may be used or reproduced in
any manner whatsoever without written permission of
the publishers except brief quotations embodied in
critical articles or reviews. For information address
Abingdon Press, Nashville 2, Tennessee.

Library of Congress Catalog Card Number: 44-3711

F

SET UP, PRINTED, AND BOUND BY THE
PARTHENON PRESS, AT NASHVILLE,
TENNESSEE, UNITED STATES OF AMERICA

DEDICATED

to the Invisible Congregation of the

NATIONAL RADIO PULPIT

whose interest has been

my inspiration

Iт was my privilege to deliver the Fondren lectures for 1943 at Southern Methodist University. Those who heard the lectures may recall that they were given under the general title "Religion's Third Front." The original material is contained in this book, although the arrangement has been changed almost beyond recognition.

The occasion for the change of title may reveal something of the book's nature. A few years ago my friend, Dr. Alfred D. Moore, an editor of Methodist church-school literature, suggested to me the writing of a book on the American way of life. He said, "Why not use the Preamble of our Federal Constitution as a pattern and fill in the clauses with your interpretation?" Another book was under way at the time, and his letter was forgotten. At least, so I thought. Then one day when these lectures were in course of preparation there flashed into my mind, as if for the first time, the idea of using the Preamble of the Constitution as the framework for the argument. Only after these chapters were nearing completion did I accidentally run across Dr. Moore's letter. Apparently his suggestion had been buried in my subconscious.

In a sense the material of this volume is an upsurge of ideas which have long been brewing in the subliminal vat of my mind. The book is not the result of cloistered meditation but of multitudinous contacts with men in all walks of life. It does not presume to present an articulated program for the postwar world. It merely gives the viewpoint of one private citizen as he looks out on the American scene in this hour of supreme crisis.

7

The task of our generation is to keep faith with the greatness of those who have gone before us so that we shall not betray those who come after us. The fundamental principles bequeathed to us by the Founding Fathers must now be projected into the frontiers of the future. Our youth do not know what kind of world they will be living in tomorrow, but every youth of twelve years or over should know what kind of person he wishes to be tomorrow and in the days after tomorrow. The war is changing the conditions of living, but not the goals of life or the patterns of personality. This book aims to lift the enduring objectives and standards of our democratic way of life above the smoke of battle and the blueprints of postwar reconstruction.

Even the longest journey has to begin with the first step. This is a book of first steps. I have therefore tried to suggest some of the squad movements which we can execute on our local drill grounds in preparation for moving up to the complex front-line problems of industrial justice, racial brotherhood, and world peace. Experts will sit at the peace table, but we common people sit at our dinner tables. And it is in the home conversations, the school curriculums, the church worship and forums that the atmosphere is to be created which will make effective the programs of the peace planners. This volume is concerned with the creation of atmosphere. We must get religion into the air of our living if we are to have a righteous America.

While the scope of the book is vast, the treatment is limited to the points of sharpest tension. The issues which seem central to the writer may appear peripheral to the reader. But if this selection starts the reader to thinking about pertinent problems which have been omitted, the value of the book will have been increased.

This is not another war book, nor is it designed to be a discussion of the coming peace. The Negro minister made a wise observation when he said, "It now looks as if the duration would last longer than the war." The unsettlement after the guns cease firing may present the severest test of our civilization. I have tried to project my thinking through the "duration" to those continuing tasks which will eventually make ours a nation Christian in culture as well as in name.

I have written frankly from the standpoint of one who calls himself a Christian. This is done in no narrow or sectarian attitude. But I believe that the spirit of Christ, if we can really catch it, is broad enough to embrace the elements essential to "life, liberty, and the pursuit of happiness."

I desire to express my deep appreciation to Mrs. W. W. Fondren, who with her husband made the lectureship possible, and who by her presence throughout the lectures helped to make their delivery an enjoyable experience; to Dean Eugene B. Hawk, President Umphrey Lee, and other members of the Southern Methodist University faculty for their characteristically gracious hospitality; to Mrs. Elmer E. Count, Mrs. Helen Hiller Palmer, Miss Betty Ohori, and my patient, efficient secretary, Mrs. Helen V. Putnam, for their valuable assistance in preparing the manuscript.

RALPH W. SOCKMAN

CONTENTS

PREAMBLE

Madame Roland's apostrophe to liberty could with equal appropriateness be addressed to destiny. "O Destiny! how many crimes are committed in thy name!" Napoleon following his star of destiny across the corpses of his countrymen, Fichte asserting that the superiority of German civilization is rooted in the external order, expansionist politicians seeking popular votes by prating about America's "manifest destiny" —thus men draw blueprints of their own desires and try to conceal their autographs under the initials of divinity. The concept of destiny has served as the mirage of the dreamer, the slogan of the demagogue, and the tool of the tyrant. It is little wonder that the sound of the word arouses the suspicion, and sometimes the scorn, of sane men.

The mind of man is haunted by the persistent idea that

> There's a divinity that shapes our ends,
> Rough-hew them how we will.

With some this belief has hardened into determinism which holds man powerless to shape the patterns of his life, since whatever he thinks to be his own contribution is really the resultant of external forces playing upon him. If these forces are regarded as chaotic, then determinism dissolves into an "accidental collocation of atoms." If man's external master be thought of as theistic, then we have the doctrine of predestination. Or these outer controls may be viewed as im-

13

personal and naturalistic, and then we have mechanistic materialism. The trend of intelligent thought, however, has led away from these rigid deterministic theories.

But while scientific thought has been rescuing the concept of destiny from the clutches of determinism, popular thought has been betraying it into an emotional fatalism. Contact with youth today reveals how prevalent is the view that we are the slaves of fate and not masters of it. A chaplain, serving on a convoy ship and thereby sharing the confidences of many soldiers, declared recently in private conversation that there will be at least eight million fatalists in the United States after the war. A typical view is thus expressed: "When the bullet or bomb comes along with my number on it, it will get me, no matter what I do. Until then, why worry?" One can understand why youth, caught in a war which they did not cause and in a sea of tragic circumstances too deep for them to fathom, should accept certain fatalistic views; and one feels disinclined to criticize men in the danger zones of war who find release from fear in such a carefree philosophy. But while fatalism may give a certain debonair freedom from fear, it also encourages a dangerous freedom from responsibility. Suppose a sailor on a blacked-out ship, trusting to his fatalistic views that he is safe until the bomb or torpedo with his number on it comes along, lights his pipe on the open deck and so provides a target for a lurking submarine. Is he playing fair with his shipmates?

Fatalism is not a working philosophy in either war or peace. It is dangerous for the people to deaden the nerves of foresight by blind reliance on fate, just as it is dangerous for the dictator to feed his egoism by undiscriminating trust in destiny.

The fallacy of fatalistic and deterministic theories of conduct can quickly be punctured if we apply them to our enemies. However we may excuse ourselves as helpless pawns, we are not inclined to exonerate our enemies so easily. Even devout believers in predestination are not inclined to say that aeons ago, before the foundations of the earth, it was divinely foreordained that in the year 1933 a man named Adolf Hitler would become chancellor of Germany and lead his people into a global war, and that therefore he is but a tool of destiny, devoid of personal responsibility and blame.

We recognize that Hitler is partly the product of circumstance, that he was caught in a chain of cause and effect not entirely of his forging; but that chain of sequence was not forged wholly on the divine anvil. Even we of America helped to shape the events which evolved a Hitler. Our honesty of judgment and our sense of outraged justice will not allow us to explain Hitler as the product of a rigid and divine foreordination. Nor is it probable that the disciples of Bertrand Russell would be willing to apply to Hitler their master's formula and accept the Fuehrer as "the product of causes which had no prevision of the end they were achieving" and go on to say that "his origin, his growth, his hopes and fears, his loves and beliefs, are but the outcome of accidental collocations of atoms."

However popular superficial theories of fatalism may be in wartime, the doctrines of rigid determinism and blind fate receive their *coup de grâce* at the hands of the warmakers. If we really believed that our fellow men were fated to do what they do, we could not be aroused to fight them. War, though it temporarily and tragically limits man's liberty, is itself born of belief in man's moral freedom and responsibility.

How, then, shall we think of destiny? The ancient Romans held a belief in three Fates who dwelt in the deep abyss of Demogorgon and with unwearied fingers drew out the threads of life. The Norse mythology also had its three Norns or Fates. Orientals make much of kismet. And we might modernize the concept and say with an eminent Columbia professor, Dr. Frederic Petersen, that there are three sets of fates which affect the development of our lives. The first presides over our physical happenings, such as accidents, injuries, disaster, disease, death, and the like. The second plays upon us through heredity. And the third fate is the racial and social environment in which our lot is cast. The reality of these external controls can hardly be denied. Accidents and disaster do come often through no fault of the persons whom they befall. A person cannot control what his grandfather did before his father was born, yet the sour grapes which the fathers ate do set the children's teeth on edge. And the boy born with a black skin or in the gashouse district does face handicaps which he did not bring on himself.

Nevertheless, however formative be the forces which play upon us from without, there are some points at which each of us has the power and responsibility of channeling these external forces. Our setting may be blocked out by heredity, and our circumstances may be molded by a million mallet blows from outside; but we are not passive clay on the Potter's wheel. We have an inner resilience that is decisive. We are caught in movements beyond our control, movements too large for us to see the end from the beginning or all the links of cause and effect lying between; yet we are not helpless pawns moved across the chessboard of life by an invisible Player. We are "workers together with him."

DAYS OF DESTINY

Some of us remember the school days when we were set to memorizing the "decisive" battles of the world's history.

Now with clearer insight we see that the course of history does not turn on definite pivots which can be marked with precise dates. We recognize that the struggles at Thermopylae and Waterloo were not the factors which decided the shape of things to follow, but that battles are rather the volcanic eruptions of society-shaping forces whose nature must be looked for beneath the surface of military tactics. We have come to interpret history more in terms of general movements than in the movements of generals. We pay more attention to economic causes and cultural trends than to the careers of kings. We view progress less as a parade of events marshaled by spectacular personalities and more as a stream of tendencies whose culture is determined by the terrain of general culture.

Nevertheless, this broadened and deepened interpretation of history does not erase all the red-letter days from our calendars or remove from all leaders the deserved title "men of destiny." In the stream of events there come floods which sweep away old landmarks and change the course of national cultures. A rain of ideas may keep falling steadily and gently on the uplands of men's minds until the currents converge and the flood is on. Change may come gradually, "first the blade, then the ear, after that the full corn in the ear"; but change may also come suddenly "as the lightning cometh out of the east, and shineth even unto the west."

There is such a phenomenon as "the fullness of the time." Following Paul's line of thought, Christians see a long cultivation of the Hebrew culture under the stern schoolmaster of law, until "when the fullness of time was come, God sent forth his Son." And then, including Paul's career in their perspective, Christians see a further manifestation of divine timing in the preparation made by the Roman Empire through its systems of roads and laws, which enabled the gospel of the Son to be propagated. Christians, therefore, feel justified in thinking that there was a strategic conjunction of times and the Man.

Nor do we Americans need to feel sentimentally old-fashioned when we speak of certain periods in our history as days of destiny, and certain personalities as men of destiny. Washington, for example, is not to be explained as a paragon of virtue miraculously dropped by divine fiat into the midst of a chaotic colonial situation. Neither is his formative influence to be accounted for by surpassing military genius. Washington's campaigns were pretty much a succession of retreats. He lost most of his battles, but he won the revolution. And he won because he lined up with forces deeper than those recognized by the reactionaries he opposed or by the rabble he led. If he had been born a hundred years earlier, Washington would probably have been merely the gentleman friend of some colonial governor; if born a century later, Washington, with his thrift and wealth, might have been a mere moneyed magnate in the gilded era of the 1880's. But the qualities of dignity and stability which might have made Washington static in quieter times proved a rallying center for the hopes of his disorganized countrymen in the chaotic days of 1776. His was the case of a man matched with an hour.

> There is a tide in the affairs of men,
> Which taken at the flood, leads on to fortune.

But pause a moment. France felt the same tidal wave of emancipation which swept North America in the last quarter of the eighteenth century. In France the spirit of revolution resulted in an Age of Reason, a Reign of Terror, and

then a new dictatorship under Napoleon. In America the tide
of revolt led to a Constitution regarded as an enduring model
of free government and to a republic now the most powerful
in the world. In each land the new regime was "conceived in
liberty and dedicated to the proposition that all men are
created equal." What, then, made the difference? Factors too
numerous for discussion here, but the assets of this new nation would have been dissipated if there had not been men
able to match the hour of challenge.

Yes, there are "men of destiny" and "decisive hours." Although these terms have been ludicrously and lamentably
abused, let us not abandon them. The proneness to false alarms
should cause watchmen to look more closely before they raise
the cry of a new crisis, but the prophets of God were never
made mute by the mistakes of preceding predictions.

AND NOW OUR DATE

Recently a college president declared in heartening fashion
that this distress of the present is the sign of a dawn. He
cited the incident of a traveler in the Swiss Alps who spent
the night with his guide in a chalet well up in the mountains.
In the early hours of the morning he was awakened by ter-
rific crashings and rumblings. Frightened, he aroused his
guide and asked, "What is happening? Is the world coming
to an end?" Calmly the guide answered: "No. You see,
when the sun starts coming up on the other side of the mountain, its rays touch the snow at the peak, causing it to hurtle
down into the valley. Then the warming rays play upon the
surface of the glacier and cause the ice to crack with loud
reports. This is what you hear. It is not the end of the world;
it is only the dawn of a new day."

When that interpretation of our time was repeated in the

VERNON REGIONAL
JUNIOR COLLEGE LIBRARY

presence of Bishop Francis McConnell, he said that this talk
about the dawn of a new day reminded him of an experience
which he had when he left his Brooklyn pastorate to become
president of DePauw University at Greencastle, Indiana,
some thirty miles west of Indianapolis. He thought that, inas-
much as he was going to live in a small city, he would in-
dulge in his long-cherished dream of having a poultry yard.
This he did. Then to his surprise he found that the rooster
crowed each morning at two o'clock. He could not understand
this phenomenon, for he had been led to believe that what
caused cocks to crow was their animal prescience by which
they detected the first rays of the dawn. Therefore he decided
to stay and watch. And, surely enough, at two o'clock in the
morning the cock crowed lustily. "But," says Bishop Mc-
Connell, "I discovered that what made the rooster crow was
not the first rays of the dawn but the headlight of the last
interurban car from Indianapolis coming around the corner."

We must not fool ourselves by mistaking every passing headlight for the dawn of a new day. Nor must we fool ourselves
by assuming that every crash of defeat is the crack of doom.
We would be realistic. But the more intense realism of our
times is one of the reasons which warrant us in calling this
a day of destiny. Unlike the soldiers of twenty-five years ago,
our troops are not going forth to battle believing this to be a
war to end war and a struggle to make the world safe for
democracy. We know now that wars are not ended by war,
and we have been led to a deeper questioning of what makes
democracy safe, even for ourselves, to say nothing of the rest
of the world. But in this abandonment of shallow optimism
about war and in this deeper skepticism about democracy
lies, in part, our hope for a new day.

There is a new tonal depth to the interpretations of our

time. Let us listen to a quartet of voices drawn from the
background of four different national cultures. Thomas Mann,
writing while the war clouds were gathering, but before the
storm actually broke, said: "Outwardly we live in an epoch
of retrograde civilization, wherein treaties are worthless, law-
lessness and disloyalty are the contagious mode. But there is an
inward spirit among men which has entered upon a new
moral epoch: one of simplification, of humble-minded recognition of the difference between good and evil. That is *its*
way of returning to the primitive and renewing its youth." [1]
Thus speaks perhaps the greatest living German, himself a
victim of his own nation's convulsions. He sees the elemental
barbarism bared by the upheaval, but through it all he sees
the possibility of moral simplification and spiritual renewal.

Put alongside this word of Thomas Mann the thesis of
P. A. Sorokin, the Russian, now chairman of the department
of sociology at Harvard. His contention is that we are now
witnessing the final stages of disintegration in what he calls
our "sensate culture." During the Christian era Western culture has gone through three stages. First, the "ideational"
culture, in which the supersensory and the suprarational were
treated as the only true reality and value. About the twelfth
century this began to decline and was superseded by an
"idealistic" culture, which blended the other-worldly and the
this-worldly. During its dominance in the thirteenth and four-
teenth centuries interest in earthly affairs began to be empha-
sized, but only in their heroic and godlike aspects. But the
concerns of this world, once welcomed into the vestibule of
the Western mind, began to fill the whole house of thought.
Thus developed a "sensate" culture, which has written great
chapters of material and social progress since the sixteenth

[1] "Culture and Politics," *Survey Graphic*, February, 1939, p. 151.

not precisely in 1940, for epochs do not start on definite dates. It was dawning perhaps as far back as 1914. It must not repeat the error which has vitiated "modern times." The vice of modernity has been a lust for abandonment, a worship of change and relativity to the point where it ceased to discriminate between the outworn and the eternal. "The new era will be founded on that discrimination." [4]

This war is not a melodrama but a tragedy. Unlike a melodrama, this conflict will not end with everything turning out right according to the success patterns of the spectator —with the villains punished and the heroes ready to live happily ever afterward. Not even the victors will see a return to the neat normalcies expected from prewar precedents. This war is a tragedy on a world stage; and in a tragedy of the Greek or Shakespearian type, the characters confront factors of destiny too deep for them to fathom and too great for the action of the drama to resolve. In *Romeo and Juliet*, Juliet dies, but not until she has revealed the grandeur of a love which overreaches the marital state. Othello drives a dagger into his own breast, but not until he has demonstrated a depth of contrition and a magnanimity of spirit which make his physical death seem almost incidental.

If both the victors and the vanquished come out of this war humbly recognizing that they must reckon with forces of destiny too great for their clever manipulation, then they will be in the mood to lay the foundations of a just and durable peace. If we can delve below the renascent barbarism to what Mann sees as the spirit of inner moral renewal; if our "sensate" culture, as Sorokin terms it, can reach up to recapture its soul; if agonized voices like that of Noyes can call our secularized specialists back from the edge of the

[4] *What Man Can Make of Man,* Harper & Bros., 1942, p. 19.

abyss to main highroads of the spirit; if with Hocking we can turn the tide of modernity from the latest thing to the lasting things—then we shall be on the way to keep our date with destiny.

How long our world will remain in its present plastic state we can only conjecture. We do know, however, that the faster the potter's wheel turns, the swifter the drying process. The hands that would shape the pattern of things to come must work fast. Twenty years ago a few thousand determined Frenchmen could have forestalled the present pitiable state of France. Today consecrated minorities can do what it may cost millions of lives to do twenty years hence. Reforms which would require a century of ordinary existence can now be wrought in a decade.

Yet even more imperative than speed of action is an accurate sense of direction. The exhaustion of the last war was followed by dynamic drives, but in the wrong directions. Perhaps the most visibly vigorous at the start was the frenzy for fascism, which has already been frustrated. "Mussolini was deposed not by the king or the army, but by defeat. The only opposition he had not killed in twenty years of one-party rule was the opposition of events, and history was the enemy that at last destroyed him." [5]

We may fail to keep our date with destiny; but, as Lincoln said, we cannot escape history.

[5] Anne O'Hare McCormick, *New York Times,* July 31, 1943.

We the People of the United States

Bigness may blight as well as inspire. We the people of the United States take justifiable pride in the energy and enterprise which have lifted thirteen struggling colonies into a nation numbering more than a hundred and thirty millions. We naturally are thrilled that the prime minister of the country from which we cast ourselves off now hails us as "in many ways the leading community in the civilized world." [1]

Yet individual personality hardly seems to count so potently in our expanded country as it did in the little nation of our Founding Fathers. When we look back to the beginnings of our government, the human relationships appear so simple and personal. Our national institutions seem the lengthened shadows of certain individuals. Whereas the financial operations of our Continental Congress were so small that the personal fortunes of Washington and Robert Morris helped to stabilize them, we now adopt budgets of sixty or more billions. Whereas the population of these United States in 1790 was only 3,929,214, we now have over three million employed in running the machinery of government. Amid the vastness of administrative bureaus the contribution of the individual seems insignificant. When we are mobilizing armies of ten or twelve millions, what mean a few lives more or less?

[1] Winston Churchill, Address at Harvard University, September 6, 1943.

Thus we are now challenged by the task of counteracting the blight of the bigness which we boast.

As the group grows, the individual tends to shrink. The temptation is to be somewhat less of a man in a city of seven million than in a town of seven thousand or a village of seven hundred. In the little community of my boyhood a young man had many incentives to keep in the straight and narrow path. He was known to all he met. He felt his efforts counted. But in a city like New York there are no neighborhood newspapers to keep track of his virtues and no neighborhood gossips to keep track of his vices. And what does his vote or influence matter among the millions who mill through the streets? For this reason the civic and moral life of a large city is usually at a lower per capita level than that in a small community. Individuals who were useful citizens in their home towns are sent to the headquarters of business in large cities, and there they shelve their community responsibilities and become spectators of the passing show. Thus potential leadership is paralyzed where it is needed most, and the individual is lost in the darkness of the crowd.

Can we the people of the United States preserve the individual from being dwarfed by the growing pressure of numbers? Guizot, the French historian, once asked James Russell Lowell how long the American republic would endure. Lowell replied that it would last as long as the ideas of the men who founded it continued dominant. In a democracy the continued dominance of ideas and ideals is not guaranteed by any divinely appointed apostolic succession of inspired leaders. It depends on the ability to get these ideas and ideals into the channels of culture which shape the attitudes of common men. Ideas and ideals must be related to activities and standards. An ideal is something we reach for; a standard is something we take hold of. And unless we have something to take hold of, eventually the ideal vanishes.

THE CREATORS OF ATMOSPHERE

However large the group in which he is engulfed, the individual is a creator of atmosphere. Even the least of us carries an aura of influence. Everyone "has an air about him," indefinable as it may be. And when a person becomes charged with a purpose or a passion, his power of radiation expands. Personal enthusiasm is so contagious and kindling that a man aglow with faith can move crowds which are left cold by the greater plans of a man who lacks zeal. Devout attachment to a good cause imparts a magnetism even to a man of mediocre ability. It was to a company of very modestly equipped men that Christ said, "Ye are the salt of the earth." Yet they proved to have that pervasive quality characteristic of salt. Because of the "boldness" of Peter and John, the people of Jerusalem took notice of them. And that courageous passion, caught from their crucified Leader, went on permeating the Mediterranean world, until within six centuries the church became the one power able to take over the remnants of the decadent Roman Empire. The primitive artists had a correct instinct when they painted halos around the heads of the apostolic saints to symbolize the aura of influence radiated by consecrated living.

This obvious old truth of individual influence has now a new social warrant for arresting our attention. The power of personal influence must be developed to save us from the perils of professional propaganda. The radio, the press, and the motion picture have vastly magnified the power of the propagandist. The radio, especially, gives a sounding board to the demagogue, as shown by the popular effect of Hitler's fervid oratory and the fanatical appeals of certain eccentric religious cults. But while the less thoughtful crowds are caught by the specious slogans of the demagogue, educated persons are so suspicious of propaganda that they look for it behind every headline, every microphone, even every pulpit. The sophisticated pride themselves that "nobody can put anything over on us." Thus develops a dangerous social situation in which islands of aloof and inert intellectuals are surrounded by the choppy seas of crowd thinking, which can easily be whipped into destructive storms.

And how are the intellectual groups to be aroused from their inertia? Not by impassioned appeals for sane thinking to counteract the herd-mindedness of the crowd. For one thing, sane thinking is not stimulated by perfervid appeals; and for another, there is altogether too much academic snobbery which scorns all common men as morons. We do not create clear thinking by merely denouncing prejudice, for prejudice is an evil which everybody denounces and nobody thinks he has. We must stir the thoughtful to social participation and leadership by means consonant with freedom of thought. We must rely less on the methods of direct persuasion and more on the free and open sharing of ideas in conversation and forums. Independent thinkers resent having formulas of action put over on them, but they welcome facts put over to them. And here it is that the contagion of personal indirect influence becomes effective.

Take, for illustration, the college campus, which boasts itself the habitat of free thought. A few years ago I was the chapel preacher at an Eastern college which during the preceding week had welcomed a new president. In his matriculation address the incoming president had spoken in this tenor: "I myself do not like to be regulated by a lot of rules, but there are certain conventions which gentlemen everywhere

observe. Those conventions will be observed on this campus."
These remarks registered a decided hit with the students.
Why? Not because he used the softer word "conventions"
instead of the unpleasant term "rules," but because he impressed the students as a gentleman setting a style of conduct
on the campus, without any effort to preach it down at them.
The student who is skeptical of propaganda, who dislikes to
be "preached to" because he thinks the preacher is putting
something over on him, is nevertheless responsive to the influence of a respected teacher or an admired fellow student.

The perils of propaganda must be counteracted by the style
setters of sane thinking. National broadcasts should be supplemented by local town meetings conducted in the spirit of
free and fair sharing of ideas. The churches, if they would
free themselves from stodgy conventionality and enlist the
minds of the most thoughtful, must return to the apostolic
secret of contagious power, which was the sharing of experience. The earliest church was merely a company of the friends
of Jesus, each telling what he knew about his Lord. Later
developed that professionalism which was to prove so paralyz-
ing. Today the conventional church is a professional propaganda agency, financed by silent spectators; preachers are hired
to preach the sermons, musicians are hired to express the
emotions, evangelists are engaged to recruit the members,
while the laity simply sit back and pay the bills—and some
just sit back.

We have become victims of the cult of publicity as well as
of propaganda. We have come to count so much on spectacular personages that we neglect the creative influence of the
common man. When a war-bond sale is to be launched, we
bring to a city the glamorous figures of the screen or famous
heroes of the battlefield. This is all very well, provided we the

people do not become mere supine spectators of the spectacular. Morale is stimulated by "stars" who display exceptional courage, but it is far better sustained by the common folk who have the power of encouragement. In *The Virginian* Owen Wister makes the uncultured cowboy say: "It was neither preaching nor praying that made a better man of me, but one or two people who believed in me better than I deserved, and I hated to disappoint them."

We the people are called to be the creators of atmosphere. We, individually, are summoned to be the pace setters of serious and intelligent thinking. We, individually, must be the centers of encouragement if morale is to be preserved. We cannot offer our insignificance as an alibi for our inaction. Each of us, even the least, does count. In a world as plastic as ours, the impact of every individual is a shaping influence. Our conversations, our unconscious attitudes, create atmosphere. Each day offers some opportunity to every one of us for affecting the racial attitudes and social outlooks of those around us. Every week gives some chance to advance the peacemaking spirit.

In a recent speech Winston Churchill recalled Count Ciano's reported defense of Italy's attack on fallen France, which was that "such a chance would not occur again in five thousand years." Then Mr. Churchill added this comment: "Certainly in June, 1940, the odds and the omens seemed very favorable to fascist ambition and greed. It is not given to the cleverest and the most calculating immortals to know with certainty what is their interest. Yet it is given to quite a lot of simple folk to know each day what is their duty." [2]

The strength of a nation is in such simple folk to whom it is given to know each day what is their duty.

[2] Speech delivered at Quebec, August 30, 1943.

THE CELLS OF CULTURE

The individual is not only a creator of atmosphere through his own personality but constitutes a cell in the organism of society. Naturally the rugged individualist has not given due emphasis to the principle of the organism in social improvement; and, strangely enough, socialistic literature has ignored some of the most formative phases of the organic principle.

Consider the first social organism in which the individual functions—the home. A home has individuality. It has an atmosphere. It is more than the sum of the members. It is a living organism. And one member can often change the atmosphere of a whole household. One boy in a mountain cabin catches the desire for an education, and the whole family is lifted from squalor to decency. One daughter in a worldly home is thoroughly converted to the Christian way of life; and ere long the family is functioning in a Christian manner, even though the other members have not accepted Christianity. Thus the individual as a cell in the family organism grows unpredictably in influence.

The climate of the home, more than any other single factor, conditions the atmosphere of culture. Time is on the side of the family. The church, at best, has the child perhaps one hour a week; the day school conditions him for some forty hours; and his other fifty or sixty waking hours are at the disposal of his home environment. Here develop naturally the situations which shape his lifelong attitudes—consideration for other personalities, recognition of rightful authority, respect for other races, interest in world affairs. And now with the radio bringing the news, the art, the voices of world leaders, even the modest home has the opportunity of weaving the richest strands of culture into the texture of growing character.

Homemaking must be studied and developed in the light

of its enlarging social significance. When we face a long-range social problem, such as the abolition of war or the improvement of race relations, we say: "The only hope lies in our children, for we cannot teach an old dog new tricks. We must therefore educate the young." Then we give ourselves so lackadaisically to child training that the little dogs learn by imitation the bad tricks of the oldsters before we teach them the new thought patterns. In Sinclair Lewis' *Main Street* the young mother, rebelling against the provincialism of Gopher Prairie, points to the fuzzy head of her little daughter and says to her phlegmatic husband: "Do you know what that is? It's a bomb to blow up smugness." But the explosion so seldom comes off, because the child-bombs become buried too deeply in the engulfing smugness. Thus continue the vicious circles of provincial pettiness, race prejudice, persistent injustice, and recurring wars.

We the people of the United States could recondition the atmosphere of our whole country within a decade if we were to treat the religious and cultural ideals of the democratic way of life with the formula enjoined upon ancient Israel: "And these words, which I command thee this day, shall be in thine heart: and thou shalt teach them diligently unto thy children, and shalt talk of them when thou sittest in thine house, and when thou walkest by the way, and when thou liest down, and when thou risest up. . . . And thou shalt write them upon the posts of thy house, and on thy gates." If we were to lift the conversations of our homes to spiritual levels; if we were to relate our religious beliefs to our secular affairs in simple, straightforward, matter-of-fact language; if we were to follow the news broadcasts with family discussions which develop world outlooks into world sympathies; if we were to make our households partnerships of free minds in which the experiences of the elders supplement the experiments of the young-sters—then we would realize the unused cultural and religious possibilities of the home.

While the home is the first and most formative organism in which the individual functions as a cell, it is only one illustration of the principle that personal influence can be immeasurably extended through utilization of the group. Being recently so impressed by the thesis that moral man exists in an immoral society, we have stressed the indubitable fact that personal morality is frequently and tragically thwarted by group immorality. Now perhaps it is time to emphasize the obverse, that personal morality can so leaven the group that its collective action is on a higher plane than the attitudes of many an individual within it. Mr. Chips lifts the tone of Brookfield School so that it vibrates to a higher pitch than the morals of many a boy in it. One dynamically Christian member of a business firm can create a Christian spirit of corporate action even though many of his fellow directors remain hard-fisted men of the world. A half-dozen devout souls can deepen the spiritual life of a whole church, although half a hundred hypocrites sit in the pews. And, likewise, a creative minority can so permeate the atmosphere of a nation as large as ours that America in her corporate action could merit the title of a Christian nation.

If a wicked minority can pervert national action—as was the case with the Nazi Party in Germany, the Fascist group in Italy, and the military clique in Japan—why cannot a godly minority convert a nation's governmental attitude? It can, provided it cares enough to be creative.

Let us not join the chorus of reactionaries who say that there is no use in attempting social reforms until we Christianize the individuals who have to make them work. That attitude would postpone improvement indefinitely—which is often what its advocates desire. While it is true that a new atmosphere must be created in order to make reforms work, it is also true that the attempt to make them work helps to create the atmosphere. The conversion of systems and souls can and must work concurrently.

In moral cultivation the group is the natural unit. Virtues are acquired through functioning in life situations and become effective in group settings. Habits are not attitudes which can be carried around as a plumber carries his kit of tools, to be used wherever there is a moral leak. The individual is a cell in the various social organisms wherein he lives and moves and has his being.

And in our present situation it is the smaller group organisms which most imperatively call for attention. When national and international organizations are disrupted, the maintenance of stability in local spheres of action becomes doubly important. And these local points of need are the ones least likely to receive attention in a time which turns men's thoughts to world problems. The present popular attitude recalls the proverb: "Wisdom is before him that hath understanding; but the eyes of a fool are in the ends of the earth." Large outlooks may easily lessen local application. We are like soldiers in a training camp, impatient with the routine of squad drills and eager to move up to front-line action. But unless we do our less colorful work on the local drill grounds of the home, the school, the parish church, the community organizations, we shall not attack effectively the large problems of industrial conflict, racial tension, international disorder. Unless we can learn to deal justly with our Harlems and Detroits, we can hardly expect to settle satisfactorily the future status of Burma and India. Until we can bridge the class distinctions in our local church congregations, we can scarcely hope to spread democracy over the globe. Unless we can develop more comity among the churches along Main Street and further organic union among our denominations, we Christians are not very convincing advocates of a united world.

If we are to keep our date with destiny, we the people need a bifocal vision. We must catch the long-range views of our world problems and our ultimate goals. We must also sharpen our vision of things near by in order to develop the insight, the sympathy, the discipline, the sureness of touch necessary to make our ideals effective.

THE COMMON MEN OF DESTINY

When we speak of men of destiny, our thoughts turn at once to the great formative figures of history. They shaped events. They were men with a mission. But both our conventional Christianity and our traditional democracy have failed to bring the sense of divine mission down to the man on the street.

But why cannot the common man be inspired to feel that he too is a man with a mission? "God is no respecter of persons." The good news of the Christian gospel is that the heavenly Father, who has his eye on the sparrow, is concerned for the value of each individual. If every leaf on the tree has its own individuality, if every human fingertip has its distinctive configuration, is it beyond belief to follow the implication of divine love to the conviction that every human being has a mission, a destiny? Yet in popular thought this sense of divine vocation is still reserved for the spiritual aristocracy.

Stanley Jones, returning to America from his work in India shortly before Pearl Harbor, declared that the present generation of American youth is the finest our country has produced, taller in body, better trained in mind; but he asserted that it lacks one vital thing—a sense of mission. He asked a group of college students what they considered to be their mission in life. They were silent for a time. Then one student ventured the answer that their aim was "to get ahead in life." Dr. Jones said that he told this incident to a company of businessmen, and they could see little wrong with the reply.

Persons motivated by the aim of "getting ahead in the world" differ from men with a sense of mission as a suburban local train differs from the Twentieth Century Limited. While the man with a mission dashes ahead on the long pull toward a distant goal, the person who wants merely to "get ahead" steams along with intermittent starts and stops. He may desire to do his work well, to make a good living for his family, to educate his children, to leave a worthy reputation at the end. But in all this he is far from the sense of propulsion which made Paul say, "I follow after, if that I may apprehend that for which also I am apprehended of Christ Jesus." Using individual will power to follow ideals is something less than being used of God in purposes which run beyond oneself.

The new era which we are now entering has been called "the century of the common man." The implication is that the dignity and value of the plain citizen are about to receive their long-overdue recognition. But this devoutly desired goal cannot be attained without a democratizing of the sense of mission. The common man must accept his Bill of Responsibilities as well as claim his Bill of Rights. We cannot healthily have government for the people unless it is a government by the people.

Mere exhortation to take more interest in public affairs is not enough to arouse the common man. Civic responsibilities must be made sufficiently simple and concrete for the individ-

ual to find places to take hold. In the conduct of war we suc‑
ceed in doing this. We create so many points of contact with
the war machine that every least member of the common‑
wealth feels that he can do something. But when we turn from
war to the promotion of peace or the creation of civic spirit,
the task seems so nebulous that the individual says to himself
helplessly, "But what can one insignificant person do about it?"
In war we the people put our shoulders to the wheel; in peace
we shrug our shoulders.

Esther Forbes in *Paul Revere* reminds us that when the
Continental army was disbanded after Yorktown the soldiers
found no place to fit themselves into the peacetime economy.
At first they were patient in their idleness; then they became
restless, even rebellious. It was in that period that the word
"soldiering" came into our language as a term of contempt.
It is a vivid commentary on our civic mismanagement that in
war the word "soldier" carries the picture of devotion, in‑
dustry, sacrifice, while in peace the word "soldiering" connotes
just the opposite—shiftlessness, lack of interest, the killing of
time. Shall we repeat the tragedy; shall we in our days of
demobilization turn again from soldiers to "soldiering"?

But the enlistment of the common man in civic responsi‑
bilities does not depend wholly on making these responsibilities
simple and concrete. A spirit of devotion and enthusiasm is
also required. Some years ago a dean at Wellesley said: "Dur‑
ing the World War the girls on this campus developed a unity
of spirit and an intensity of co-operation which were a delight
to behold, despite the overhanging shadows of war's cruelty.
Do you think any such situation can be duplicated in peacetime for peace purposes?" Well, if we cannot develop a com‑
parable unity and consecration in peace causes, then wars will
go on. Civic responsibilities must be made as all-consuming,

if not as colorful, as military service. In war we personalize our country, and on our war posters we portray her as a mother endangered or in distress. When peace comes we depersonalize our "mother country" into "the government"; we change the pronoun from "her" to "its"; and the adjectives we use depend on our politics. Thus patriotism loses both its colorfulness and its appeal in peacetime. If this is to be the century of the common man, he must make it so by the public service he renders and not merely by the public service he hopes to receive.

One of the noblest figures that emerged from the first World War was G. A. Studdert-Kennedy, a British chaplain who strove with bravery during the war and then fought with equal gallantry to save the ideals of the peace afterward. Before he died this high-minded soul declared that the most searching question which he expected to face at the final Judgment Day would be this: "What did you make of it?" What question could be more in tune with the teachings of Christ and more inclusive of his purpose? And it is a question to sting our consciences awake. We are privileged to live in a fateful hour when world society is fluid as never before, when reforms can be realized quickly which in ordinary times might require centuries. How, then, shall we answer the question, "What did you make of it?"

form a more perfect Union

When the framers of our Federal Constitution set out "to form a more perfect union," they had in mind certain problems which no longer seem so serious to us. They were confronted with the sectional jealousies of their small but sprawling new nation. Today those rivalries are largely erased. Sectional differences due to diversity of economic, political, and religious thought still exist; but in situations calling for united action there is no East or West, no North or South, in these United States.

Our Founding Fathers confronted also deep cleavages between the states. The task of uniting the proud commonwealths of Virginia and New York and Massachusetts seemed as difficult in the 1780's as the problem of joining sovereign nations in a world government seems in the 1940's. Although the danger of secession from the Union is now happily past, the issue of states' rights versus federal control is still a pertinent one. The trend toward centralization of powers in Washington has the peril of removing government further from the people and lessening that local autonomy which invites individual participation. But these dangers do not fall within the scope of this book, and furthermore we can trust the politicians to keep the issues alive.

The disunity which threatens us goes deeper than any division between sections or between states and the federal government. One dangerous line of cleavage is social, between economic classes and between racial groups. The status of our citizenry resembles that of passengers on a ship. In normal times the passengers travel in classes: first class in the best accommodations on the upper decks, second class in the less desirable cabins lower down, and third class in the steerage. But if the ship strikes a mine, the passengers awake to the fact that they are "all in the same boat." In the perilous waters of the present war we realize that we are all in the same boat. And temporarily our divergent economic and racial groups have more or less declared a truce. But when harmony is due to the fear of a foreign foe, then beware what will happen when the danger of Japan and Germany is removed. We may see a recrudescence of industrial disturbances and racial tensions surpassing the strikes and Ku-Klux-Klanism of painful memory in the postwar period of the 1920's.

The fires of racial feeling have only been banked, and the flares which broke through in Detroit and Harlem reveal the smoldering passions with which we shall have to reckon. The rich are haunted by the fear of plots on the part of organized labor. And the cry of communism from one side is answered by the cry of fascism from the other. We still have these social chasms to bridge "in order to form a more perfect union." But of this phase we shall speak further in dealing with "domestic tranquillity."

THE FALL OF HUMPTY DUMPTY

We must go still deeper than racial and industrial relations to reach the roots of the disunity which endangers us in this day of destiny. Our whole culture has suffered disintegration.

Nursery jingles often have both rhyme and reason. When we become men, we put them away as childish things; but here is one jingle which should be resurrected from childhood's attic of memories for our adult rereading:

> Humpty Dumpty sat on a wall;
> Humpty Dumpty had a great fall;
> All the king's horses and all the king's men
> Couldn't put Humpty Dumpty together again.

It is a riddle. And the answer is that Humpty Dumpty is an egg. When an egg is broken, all the king's horses and all the dictator's forces cannot put it together again. A broken egg cannot be patched. Something new must be hatched.

And there are things other than eggs which, when broken, cannot be patched but require a new birth. When Jesus appeared in Palestine, he taught with such power and appeal that earnest leaders of Israel began to wonder whether this young carpenter could show them how to patch the breaks in their ecclesiastical structure. One scribe, Nicodemus by name, came to inquire the secret of this new teacher. Jesus cryptically replied to Nicodemus' inquiry: "Except a man be born again, he cannot see the kingdom of God." Again it is the riddle of Humpty Dumpty. Just as an egg cannot be patched, so in the life of an individual or a church there come times when a new spirit must be hatched—a new birth must be experienced.

The principle applies also to a whole social culture. When as students we trudged our way haltingly through Vergil's *Aeneid,* most of us were not aware of the cultural crisis for which that great epic was designed. Augustus Caesar was trying to restore the crumbling foundations of Roman society, which had been undermined by a vast slave population, by foreign mercenaries replacing Roman volunteers in the army, by an urban proletariat clamoring for a liberal dole, by a mounting divorce rate devitalizing the home life, by economic exploitation of the provinces making for luxury and laziness, and, most fundamentally, by a loss of the old religious sanctions. Augustus sought to create a cohesive force through the revival of a nationalistic spirit and the development of a nationalistic religion. He strove to concentrate all family and municipal loyalties about the Temple of Vesta, the supreme hearth fire. He would amalgamate all local deities into a pantheon whose heavenly head was Jupiter Capitolinus and whose earthly representatives were the Caesars. In this revival, Augustus enlisted the aid of the poet Vergil. The aim of the *Aeneid* was to undergird a political revolution and a religious reform with the zeal-inspiring episodes of Roman heroism linked with the wanderings of Aeneas. But the imperial power of Augustus plus the literary charm of Vergil could not put Rome's fallen Humpty together again. A new spirit had to be born. And in the unpropitious province of Palestine was born a new spirit, which six centuries later was to make Rome the center of a new culture.

And now Humpty has suffered his worst fall in recorded history. The material structure of men and nations lies in disorder. The map of the world has been ripped up like a jigsaw puzzle. Races are seething with unrest. More social theories have been scrapped by the present global war than by any preceding historical event. Personal philosophies have been shattered. Youth are groping among the ruins of their hopes for the lost clues of life's larger meaning.

The more perfect union which we now seek to establish must be one able to unify not only the states within our nation but the nations within the global community, for in our fluid society we can no more separate ourselves from the currents and convulsions of the world than we can stake off an oyster bed from the rise and fall of the tides. We cannot immunize

American minds to the ideologies which sweep other societies, nor can we long preserve domestic law and order in a lawless world.

The more perfect union must be one which can give synthesis and purpose to our secularized and specialized pursuits. We live like bees in a hive, but ours is a buzzing confusion while theirs is a busy construction. We have become specialists in our lines, but we are weak at weaving our lines into worthwhile patterns. We have developed a luxuriant growth of new branches on the tree of knowledge; but we have neglected the main trunk, with the result that we are trained in skills but not in that common body of knowledge which makes for wholeness of outlook and strength of character. We have drive without direction. If Aristophanes were to visit America, he would certainly repeat the verdict he pronounced upon Athenian life in the age of the Sophists, "Whirl is king, having driven out Zeus."

If we are to establish a more perfect union adequate for our day, it must be one able to unify the states of mind within the individual, so that he feels himself going somewhere and also getting somewhere. Thornton Wilder in *The Woman of Andros* pictures a young man looking into the future. The youth has come to the conclusion that most mortals merely endure the slow misery of existence. That feeling is strengthened by the fretful and unsatisfied attitude of his parents. "He was twenty-five already, that is—no longer a young man. He would soon be a husband and a father. . . . He would soon be the head of this household and this farm. He would soon be old. Time would have flowed by him like a sigh, with no plan made, no rules set, no strategy devised that would have taught him how to save these others and himself from the creeping gray, from the too-easily accepted frustration. 'How does one live?' he asked the bright sky. 'What does one do first?' " [1] To give the common man a philosophy of life which answers such longings is one function of the more perfect union which we seek.

In the spring of 1937 a French businessman came to America in a private capacity and at his own expense. As he said to one whom he interviewed, he came to find the answer to two questions. One question was this: "Can our democracies generate a fervor and devotion in their youth comparable to that which the dictatorships have kindled in their young devotees?" And the other question was: "Can an organization be developed to handle the refugee problem on an international scale similar, for instance, to the methods of the Red Cross?" These two questions reflected the disintegration both within the individual spirit and within the social structure. Youth in their freedom had lost the zest of living. Nations with their philosophy of force, their instincts of greed, their theories of race, had lost the power of living together.

"The current political and economic dislocations, culminating in the military threat of world conquest, are in large part the ultimate effects of world-wide intellectual confusion and spiritual and moral deterioration. This deterioration of standards of thought and action affected society in its most sensitive aspects—namely, the fields of art, letters, philosophy, and thought—long before the advent of the war." [2]

Within the space of a single generation we can trace the overt manifestations of this deep-seated disintegration. Thirty years ago the youth of our Western culture were summoned

[1] A. & C. Boni, 1930, p. 38

[2] Statement of the Third Annual Conference on Science, Philosophy and Religion in Their Relation to the Democratic Way of Life, *New York Times*, September 1, 1942.

with clarion calls to risk their lives for professedly great causes. On both sides of the battle lines of 1914-18 the fighters were taught to believe that the foundations of their liberty were at stake. Then when all became quiet on the western front, youth felt themselves deeply deceived. The leaders of state had cruelly misled them. The leaders of the church had piously sanctioned the specious theories of so-called sovereign states. The leaders of education had proved blind guides. And in youth's eyes even their parents, out of loyalty to false gods, had let them down. Bitterly disillusioned, youth abandoned all leaders. Then began the era of self-indulgence camouflaged as self-expression. From the ranks of regimentation they swung to a rampant individualism. With their loosened loyalties, emancipated youth became as atomistic as a sand pile.

The result was a restlessness of spirit and a general insecurity of life. Then, liberty having run from license to chaos, men began to call for a leadership which could deliver business from its morass and life from its meaninglessness. Those who had once wanted liberty without order were ready to welcome order without liberty. Thus was prepared the way for the dictators.

SOME RECENT ATTEMPTS AT UNION

The cry for co-ordination called forth several attempted answers.

Communism found in Russia a laboratory to test its power of putting Humpty together again. Its results merit respectful consideration. When one thinks how from the chaos following the collapse of the czarist regime Lenin and Stalin lifted the illiterate and inchoate millions of Russia into a union of Soviet republics so industrially dynamic and so militarily potent that it has thrown back the supposedly mightiest war machine of modern times—when one thinks of this achievement and the zeal which inspires it, one must pay high tribute to the co-ordinating power of communism.

But communism offers little hope as a cohesive force on any world scale or in any full cultural way. It is too narrowly economic in its interpretation of man's interests. Its criteria of truth and right are relative to the interests of a class. Without entering into any discussion of the demerits of communism, may we quote the testimony of one of Russia's best-informed friends, former Ambassador Joseph E. Davies. After summing up an imposing list of the Soviet regime's assets, he lists some liabilities, among them the following—and the juxtaposition seems significant:

"*Lack of Religion*—Every effort is being made to substitute worship of a man or men for the worship of God. It is one of the greatest weaknesses of this situation.

"*Mistrust Among Leaders Themselves*—The philosophy of communism justifies all acts if done in its name. There are no considerations of honor or loyalty which control as against duty to the party. The result is that there can be no confidence or faith between these men, in leadership. No man can trust another. It is a serious and basic weakness and a constant threat to existing government." [3]

The report is now published of the *rapprochement* between church and state. What may be the political reasons back of this action we do not know, but on the face of it the new and improved status of the church supports our prediction that the Russians in their heroic sacrifices are seeking sources of morale deeper than those offered by the communistic ideal.

Party loyalty is too narrow a criterion for judging right and

[3] Joseph E. Davies, *Mission to Moscow*, Simon & Schuster, 1941, p. 402.

wrong. Class loyalty is inadequate as a cohesive force in holding even a nation together. And with all respect to the fighting efficiency and heroism of our Russian allies, their methods of trial and blood purging belie any promise which their system of government might offer as the hope of a more perfect union.

Fascism has revealed its spirit in many places, even among free peoples. But in Italy it found national scope for testing its unifying power. Certainly for a time it seemed to achieve much. On a visit to Italy in 1922 I observed a land full of pride in its historic past but with little hope for its future. I waited for trains which kept no schedules; I watched a people who seemed to be idling like a halted motor. On a return visit in 1927 I could feel the thrill of energy pulsing through the populace. The industrial machine was clicking; trains were on time; youth were drilling in the streets; the proud, vibrant old Roman spirit had been revived. But in its effort to weld the strands of human interest into the strength of a totalitarian state, fascism works by the principle of suppression. Inevitably it has to limit the development of potentialities. It cannot let disturbing thoughts have free utterance, lest they undermine its autocratic authority. In order to survive, fascism must ensure that its one point of view, its one pattern of life, prevail. It must seek a single, unbreakable hardness. But the elemental human urges are as difficult to suppress as Italy's own Vesuvius.

The bombastic little Mussolini has now been blown from his balcony, Italy has surrendered, and the remains of fascism are being sifted from the ruins of the nation. Twenty years sufficed to demonstrate the defects of the fascist principle.

Nazism does not deserve consideration as a cohesive force. With its myth of a superior race and its methods of extermination, it has demonstrated destructive but not unifying power.

Hitler has been more stupid than Bismarck in failing to recognize the futility of force as a means of conciliation, for the latter was shrewd enough to see that "you can do anything in the world with bayonets except sit on them." A blitzkrieg may clear the ground, but it does not cultivate the seeds of a new culture. You cannot indoctrinate with dynamite. Hitler's Pan-Europe cannot be created by patching together the peoples he has impoverished, nor can brotherhood be formed by regimenting the relatives of those he has butchered.

The world is now disillusioned with the foregoing ideologies, which a decade ago looked alluring to so many, even in our democracies. But as men turn from the discredited Pied Pipers of regimentation, whither shall they go to find the force which can unify the individual's states of mind into coherent wholeness, give pattern to the disordered mosaics of our materialistic culture, and bring a livable brotherhood among warring nations?

Fourteen centuries ago Christianity proved itself potent enough to bring order out of the broken fragments of Rome's imperial culture. Can the Christian faith unify the complex modern world as it did medieval European society? By the thirteenth century Europe had a civilization which could be consistently termed "Christian" in the sense that it was designed and dominated by individuals and institutions calling themselves Christian and desiring to honor their God and his divine Son. Government and business, art and architecture, domestic life and social welfare were all controlled by Christ's representative, the church.[4]

The word "medieval," however, carries memories which cause our modern age to shy away from any prospect of re-

[4] For a succinct treatment of this medieval culture see Walter M. Horton, *Can Christianity Save Civilization?* Harper & Bros., 1940, chap. ii.

turning to the conditions bearing that label. Both science and democracy have become modest enough to see their limitations but not blind enough to discard their achievements. Our culture craves unity, but it must establish a more perfect union than that which medieval Europe achieved.

Profoundly we believe and frankly we assert that Christ is the supreme co-ordinator who can bring unity out of chaos. "He is prior to all, and all coheres in him." But a Christian civilization is a Christ-inspired, not a church-controlled, culture. And to achieve such a culture, we must advance on a broader front than has hitherto been tried.

RELIGION'S THIRD FRONT

In the Christian campaign of spiritual expansion, the first front was and is personal evangelism. After Andrew meets the Christ, "he first findeth his own brother Simon." "Jesus . . . findeth Philip . . . Philip findeth Nathanael." The Christian gospel began as good news leaping from lip to lip. It was a contagion of converted lives.

And when the inexplicable Man of Galilee became "that strange man on the cross," the infectious power of his influence gained mighty impetus. His frightened followers, who on the night of his crucifixion fled the city of their tragedy, were transformed into bold heralds of a triumphant Saviour. Thus the Christian movement melted its way into the heart of the cold Mediterranean world. And through nineteen centuries the followers of Christ have been going forth to "teach all nations, baptizing them in the name of the Father, and of the Son, and of the Holy Ghost." This relay race of Christ's messengers has now belted the globe, and some six hundred millions call themselves followers of his faith.

With over a fourth of the world's population already enrolled in the camp of Christ's followers, it might seem a comparatively simple matter to extend this first front of personal evangelism until, as we pray, "the kingdoms of this world shall become the kingdom of our Lord and Saviour Jesus Christ." Thirty years ago missionary leaders were talking about "the evangelization of the world in this generation," and, it did not then seem beyond possibility. But within that generation have come two world wars, both of them starting in countries called Christian.

Russia, which in my boyhood was regarded as a bulwark of the Eastern Orthodox Church, officially seceded from Christianity. Germany, to which our theological professors went for graduate study, officially repudiated the Christian church as the conscience of the state. And Italy, where the head ecclesiastical figure of Christendom resides, for twenty years followed a dictator who ran counter to the fundamental principles of the Christian faith. Therefore, despite the victories wrought by personal evangelism through the centuries, the recent record hardly warrants the hope that the world can be won for Christ on the first front alone.

One reason is that the pace of personal evangelism is too slow. If any branch of Christendom should be possessed of evangelistic zeal, it is that which sprung from John Wesley's passion for souls. Yet the record of The Methodist Church for the year 1940 shows that only 255,437 new members were brought into the fold on confession of faith. In a denomination numbering 7,336,263, this means it took approximately twenty-eight members to win one new recruit. The next year, after a unification which might have been expected to kindle an evangelistic zeal, the ratio had risen only slightly, to one recruit for every twenty-five members. If other religious groups show a somewhat similar proportional growth, it is apparent that the pace of personal evangelism hardly warrants the hope of saving the world soon enough to halt the evils now devastating the hearts and homes of men.

Furthermore, not only is the process of individual salvation too slow, but it is often inadequate in quality. The Christ who asked "Wilt thou be made whole?" was concerned to save not only the soul, with an eye to eternity, but also the whole man, with an eye to both time and eternity. But what has been termed the "saving of souls" has not always meant saving the whole personality. The conversion of the will has frequently not been followed by a cultivation of taste and thought into the formation of Christian character. And traditional evangelistic sermons have so often failed to effect Christian social attitudes. Sometime ago a young minister in Maine announced a sermon on "Saints in Cellophane." The title suggests the situation which prompted it. That socially minded young minister was no doubt exasperated by the sight of his parishioners lined up in their pews and wrapped in the protective covering of their own smugness, somewhat as cigars are neatly wrapped in cellophane and laid in a box. When cigars have reached the wrapping stage, they are all cut and dried and ready for the fire. Such might be said to be the state of "saints in cellophane."

It is a tragic waste to go on "saving souls" in Sunday school and then send them forth about once in every generation to have their bodies butchered in war. It is brutal to implant ideals in the minds of youth and then leave them to be disillusioned and morally deformed by the social systems in which they must live. Furthermore, thoughtful youth are increasingly turning deaf ears to those who would save their souls without changing the conditions of life.

Therefore, devoutly as we may desire a revival of personal

evangelism, this first front of the Christian movement is not enough to keep our date with destiny.

A second front was opened in the campaign of Christianity to win the world. It was the line commonly called the "social gospel." While this second front was started by Jesus himself and runs from the Jericho road to Main Street, the programization which the term "social gospel" suggests was begun only about two generations ago. During the closing decades of the nineteenth century the progress in technology, the expansion of commerce, the improvement of material comforts, created an atmosphere of optimism congenial to both liberal theology and social reform. Men began to preach the gospel of the Kingdom as an earthly goal and a possibility within history. The material blessings brought by the machine age could be gilded by godliness into a golden age. A social conscience was aroused. Slums were cleared. Settlement houses were established. Labor sermons were delivered. Social service departments became recognized and popular in local and national church organizations. As the years passed, the thrust of the social gospel probed more deeply from "social service" to "social action," advancing its emphasis from alleviation and settlement houses to agitation with boycotts, consumers' cooperatives, church commissions on race relations, labor, world peace, and practically every vital social issue.

The achievements of the social gospel on this second front must not be minimized in the present reaction against liberalism. It has now become the vogue to say that "the late liberals were taxidermists to a dead principle." [5] But it must not be forgotten that they did kill many birds with their stones and that it is not the principle of social action which is dead and decoratively stuffed. There are some things which Christians,

[5] Hocking, *op. cit.*, p. 44.

however soundly converted and however conscious of needing divine aid, must accomplish by social action if they are to accomplish them at all.

Yet the sanest exponents of the social gospel recognize that this second front has shown its limitations. It has all too often achieved reform without advancing to regeneration. Social reforms may succeed in putting the "ins" out and the "outs" in, in putting the "ups" down and the "downs" up, without really converting the motivations of men and the conceptions of power. The social gospel has been inclined to rely too much on the secular props of our so-called Christian civilization. It has allowed the economic concerns of man to overshadow his other cultural needs, forgetting how much life is more than meat.

Justice Felix Frankfurter, who so fought for economic reforms that he antagonized the possessors of special privilege, throws economic issues into illuminating perspective when he says: "Economics is not the whole of life. Very far from it. But on the fair and sensible control of economic forces depends the opportunity to pursue a civilized life. If only we can bring sufficient good will and resolute purpose to bear, the day need not be far off when the economic problem will take a back seat where it belongs and the arena of the heart and head will be occupied by our real problems—the problems of life and human relations, of creation and behavior and religion." [6]

There is an economic core to almost every life situation, but economics is not the center and circumference of our being. Jesus, though personally indifferent to money, was socially most mindful of it. His references to it are amazingly frequent. The Master knew how vitally monetary matters affect life, and yet he knew that man is more than an economic animal.

[6] *New York Times,* October 1, 1942.

The followers of Christ must therefore maintain this second front of the social gospel, but they must see it in clearer perspective. We must not mistake material comforts for civilization nor count on social reform to effect a spiritual regeneration. But above all we must not be driven to retreat on the social front by those old-time conservatives in the pew who never did want religion to disturb the economic *status quo* nor by the new "progressives" in the pulpit who now deem it old-fashioned to be called liberal. The "social gospel" is an integral part of the "simple gospel."

In clarifying our conception of religion's third front may we resort to a modern military analogy. The current war has demonstrated that land forces and sea forces can effectively advance and hold their gains only as they also have control of the air. Just as air control is essential to victory in war, so is it in religion. To be vital and controlling, religion must pervade the atmosphere men breathe. We must have the consciousness of God in the very air of our lives. We must come to feel that "in him we live, and move, and have our being." Using terms in a somewhat different sense from the military strategists, we may say that religion's third front is the control of the cultural atmosphere. And by the culture of a people we mean "the sum of all their activities, customs, and beliefs." [7]

In times of war the atmosphere is pervaded by the war spirit. Conversation, education, business, churches—all are conditioned by the war. What a contrast is this all-pervasiveness of war to the partial impacts of religion. "Our American culture at the present time has fallen apart into possibly seven major disciplines, each with its corresponding objectives and institutions. Science and education, economics, politics, religion, domestic and social life, sport and diversion, and art

[7] R. B. Dixon, *The Building of Cultures,* Chas. Scribner's Sons, 1928, p. 3.

have one by one emancipated themselves from the former religio-political unification, and have each projected distinct objectives and perfected separate institutions for the realization of the same." [8]

Thus religion is treated as one of numerous departments of culture. In many an academic circle it is regarded as an elective for those who "have an interest in that sort of thing." In modern art, religious themes play a very minor role, whereas in early art they furnished the chief inspiration. In economics "business is business," wherein the church is regarded as a sentimental dreamer when it dares to intrude. In politics men still accept Machiavelli's advice that the sagacious politician will always respect religion, even if he has no belief in it. In sport and diversion religion is looked upon as a Puritan kill-joy rather than as a promoter. The church makes brave pronouncements in all these areas, but there is such a woeful lag between the official statements of church conventions and the practical attitudes of church members that the resolutions are not taken seriously.

In short, religion is looked upon by the other departments of life as irrelevant rather than irreconcilable. Religion has become divorced from the other interests of living somewhat as husband and wife often become divorced. When the family situation reaches the court, the parties sue for a separation on the grounds of incompatibility; but the incompatibility developed from a separation of interests. Similarly people say that Christianity will not work in business or politics, that it is irreconcilable with science; but the underlying fact is that men have failed to relate their religious attitudes to the other aspects of life in daily practice.

[8] Archibald G. Baker, *Christian Missions and a New World Culture.* Willett, Clark & Co., 1934, p. 176.

Religion is the life of man in all his relations to God. From such relationship no area of his activity can be excluded. The church is "the bride of Christ," and she must therefore share in every interest with which he was concerned. That means the whole of life.

The hope now visible on the horizon is that leaders of thought are coming to recognize the interrelatedness of these divorced departments of culture. In 1940 there was convened in New York a Conference on Science, Religion and Philosophy in Their Relation to the Democratic Way of Life. This significant group has now held four annual conferences. In the formal statement of the third conference is this declaration: "If the malady which has produced the present disaster has its roots in every aspect of our intellectual and spiritual experience, the remedy for that malady likewise requires the co-ordination of vast fields of human experience beyond military, political, and economic interests." [9] Here at last is a group of leading scholars looking over the fences of their own special fields to seek a co-ordination of interests sufficiently wide and pervasive to change the whole atmosphere of culture. This is something more than another approach to the conflict between religion and science. It is a sign of activity and advance on religion's third front.

[9] *New York Times,* September 1, 1942.

establish Justice

Justice is the cornerstone of civilized society. Plato and Aristotle join with the Hebrew prophets in giving justice primary place in the social structure. That righteousness and justice are prerequisite to peace is a tenet of the ancient seers, the founders of our republic, and those who today look forward to a "just and durable peace."

When the father of the present Archbishop of Canterbury was headmaster of Rugby, a boy whom he had disciplined wrote a letter to his parents containing these words: "The headmaster is a beast, but he is a just beast." [1] The letter fell by accident into the headmaster's hands, and he regarded it as one of the most genuine compliments of his life, revealing as it did that his rule, however rigorous, rested on fairness. Without the foundation of justice no human relationship is safe. Charity without justice is cheap and superficial; mercy without justice is sentimental and often weakening; love without justice is a contradiction, although it is an attitude often attempted, and sad has been the wreckage thereof. [2]

In the present embittered world the Christian command to love one's neighbors, even one's enemies, seems to many a counsel of perfection, impossibly unrealistic. If we cannot attain to love, let us at least try to be fair. In our efforts to be

[1] R. H. Fisher, *Religious Experience,* Doubleday, Doran & Co., 1924, p. 242.
[2] For a further development of this theme see the author's *Highway of God,* pp. 205-10.

just we shall best build our way up to brotherly love. Here as elsewhere we shall confine ourselves to those issues in the establishment of justice which seem most critical at this juncture.

JUSTICE—INVENTION OR DISCOVERY?

The interpretation of justice has come down the centuries in two streams. One springs from the idea of justice as the mere creation of men for their mutual advantage. According to this view justice has no existence in the abstract. Man is essentially egoistic. Social and legal relations rest wholly upon individual self-interest and upon the desire of each to secure himself against injury. To the holders of such a belief, any form of political authority was satisfactory if it guaranteed peace and order. Such was the conception of justice held by the Sophists and Epicureans.

Thomas Hobbes in the seventeenth century impressively elaborated the theory. The normal condition of mankind, as he saw it, was that of unceasing strife, because of the motives of competition, distrust, and love of glory. In the natural state the hand of each is against all. There exists no distinction between right and wrong. The impulses which move men are the passions which are born in them, and there is no standard by which any one of these passions may be judged morally different from any other. Also, there is no distinction of just and unjust in the state of nature. Where there is no common power over men, Hobbes argued, there is no law, and where there is no law there can be no injustice. Justice and injustice are not faculties of the individual, like sense and emotion; and therefore they have a place, not in a consideration of the natural or solitary man, but only where men are regarded as joined by social bonds.

In contrast to this conception of justice as a mere social creation springing from self-interest is the view which may be traced from Plato. Justice is an abstract eternal ideal not deflected by the demands of a narrow and temporary expediency. It is the regulative virtue which produces a general harmony in character and general good order in conduct.

In line with Plato were the Stoics, who held justice to be immanent in nature, a form of universal reason, and therefore fixed and immutable. The ideal life was the one lived in conformity to this universal law. From the practical point of view such conformity was to be sought through the cultivation of human reason, disassociated as far as possible from emotional influence and material conditions.

Cicero carried over into Roman thought the Platonic conception of justice as eternal and unchangeable. He found for eternal justice a source in the providence of the gods, the creators of nature. Cicero argued that all nature is ruled by God. (Sometimes he used the plural but usually the singular of *deus*.) Man, the highest of created things, possesses reason and is therefore like the creator. Hence all men by nature have the consciousness of justice. Law in the true and ultimate sense is eternal wisdom ruling the world.

Augustine, who was so formative in shaping the Christian tradition, followed Cicero's view of justice with certain modifications. Augustine agreed that the source of justice is in God, but he would safeguard the assumption by insisting on belief in the true God as revealed in the Hebrew-Christian tradition.

It is essential to remind Americans that the justice which our Founding Fathers sought to establish was viewed in line with Plato and Augustine, not with Epicurus and Hobbes. It was founded on divine sovereignty and not on mere social contract.

In earlier times Christian thinkers made much of the concept of natural law. By this they did not mean a generalization from a mass of observed phenomena in the manner of modern empirical science; they meant the proper function of a human activity as apprehended by a consideration of its own nature. They studied a human activity to see if it was fulfilling the function for which it was created; we, on the other hand, keep our ears to the ground to hear the hoofbeats of the next Gallup poll and test an activity by whether it is getting the votes of the people. Consider a case in the economic field. "The reason why goods are produced is that men may satisfy their needs by consuming those goods. Production by its own natural law exists for consumption. If, then, a system comes into being in which production is regulated more by the profit obtainable for the producer than by the needs of the consumer, that system is defying the Natural Law or Natural Order." [3]

To be sure, the establishment of justice involves human reason and especially human imagination. It requires observation, experimentation, the weighing of factors. Very properly the traditional characterization of justice is a woman with a pair of scales in her hand, symbolizing the balancing of considerations which is to be effected if full justice is to be done. But we must go on to realize that it is nature's force of gravity which creates the weight to be balanced and similarly that there is something at the heart of the universe which plants the sense of justice in the mind of man. Justice is a discovery, not an invention. That belief was basic to the framers of our Federal Constitution; and to that belief we must return.

[3] William Temple, *Christianity and Social Order*, Penguin Books, 1942, p. 58.

THE QUESTION OF EQUALITY

In declaring their independence our Founding Fathers asserted their belief that all men are created equal. But in what are men equal? Saint-Exupery, the French aviator whose poetic insight has been deepened by brooding over the fate of his beloved France, writes: "It was the contemplation of God that created men who were equal, for it was in God that they were equal. This equality possessed an unmistakable significance. For we cannot be equal except we be equal in something." [4] We are equal in that each of us has the divine spark, and therefore divine dignity. We come into this world as ambassadors of God, and as such we have a right of equality of opportunity.

As a minimum, equality of opportunity means a fair start in life. Every person has a right to be physically wellborn—to be born with blood not tainted by diseased heredity, to be born to parents prepared and willing to receive him, to be born into an environment fit to provide decent bodily care.

Every person has a right to grow up in a wholesome home —a home which cushions helpless infancy with tenderness, a home in which the atmosphere of mutual trust enables the child's faculties to flower, a home which adjusts the opening eyes of childhood to the glare of the garish world.

Every individual has a right to an education which fits him with skills to make a living and with a philosophy to make a life—an education which gears the newcomer into the "on-goingness" of life, enabling him to capitalize the contributions of the past and draw interest for the future.

Every person has a right to work, for without work a person's energies turn in to destroy him. The world does not owe us a living, but it does owe us the chance to make a living.

[4] *Flight to Arras*, Reynal & Hitchcock, 1942, p. 237.

We were brought into life by others; and, up to the point where we are old enough to take over, we are guests of the society which begot us.

But does the giving of a fair start in life exhaust society's duty to provide equality of opportunity? In the race of life inequalities soon appear, for some are five-talent men and others are one-talent men. It is unfair to the former to hold them back to the pace of the latter, for that would stifle initiative and reduce living to dull regimentation. But the persons of superior talent who demand the right of free enterprise must beware lest they in their progress block the path of their slower brothers. In a horse race the fastest animal gets the inside track, thus gaining advantage over those crowded away from the rail. Similarly, in the competitive race of man with man, the quicker-witted have an inevitable advantage over the slower-paced in that they do things more efficiently and rapidly. But because of this very fact they must be the more concerned to place no hindrance to the free enterprise of the more plodding.

If we are to enjoy real equality of opportunity, the right of free enterprise must be interpreted more broadly than the mere ability of the strong to "get ahead" in the worldly materialistic sense now obtaining. There must be freedom for common men "to make the most of their common humanity." There must be opportunity for the popular enjoyment of noncompetitive things in order that men's eyes may be lifted from the commercial patterns of success and the tension of the economic drive may be lessened. One of the glories which made Periclean Athens an abiding inspiration was her democratization of her beauty and social wealth. Her buildings and her art were open for all men to enjoy, and thereby the poorest found recreation of spirit and richness of life. Differences in economic income should not, and need not, continue to make the difference they now do in personal happiness. One basic relief from the tensions now caused by monetary inequalities is to create an atmosphere in which these do not matter.[5]

THE ISSUE OF SOVEREIGNTY

It has been said that no man has a right to all his rights. This is a rather inaccurate way of asserting that all our rights have to be exercised with consideration for the rights of others.

Consider even the so-called inalienable rights of "life, liberty, and the pursuit of happiness." The man adrift on a raft with his fellow survivors may say, "I have a right to life," and while his companions sleep may take for himself the lion's share of their meager rations; but such conduct ostracizes him from the society of decent men. The soldier on picket duty, feeling that he has a right to life, may flee for safety when danger approaches; but the courtmartial takes care of such cases. The men in the Houston hotel which recently burned claimed their right to life; and by insisting on that right without regard to the others they clogged the exits, thereby causing the death of dozens. Since no man liveth to himself, every man's right to life is limited by his relationships.

Or take the "inalienable rights" of liberty and the pursuit of happiness. These have to be exercised under the constitution of the groups wherein we live. Life is a game—but not a game of solitaire. In the language of the street, we have to "play ball." The baseball player may insist that his personal liberty gives him the right to strike at the ball as often as he

[5] For further consideration of the economic aspects of equal opportunity see the next chapter.

pleases. But if he persists in doing so, he is soon left to play alone. He must yield his rights, not to the pitcher or the catcher, but to the rules of the game. Lift the principle to the sphere of the family. Marriage is a mutual surrender of prerogatives. The husband subordinates himself, not to the wife, nor she to him; both subordinate themselves to the law of love. Turn to the relationships of our federal union. The proud commonwealth of Virginia did not surrender its sovereignty to the commonwealth of New York, but both along with the other states subordinated their rights to the constitutional law of the new nation.

And now this issue of sovereignty has come to the fore in the relationship of nations. The discussion of sovereign nations and sovereign powers is becoming a major issue in political conclaves. The concept of sovereignty is in danger of being used by demagogues and politicians to wreck the hopes of a just and durable peace. The point to be kept clear is that any nation is not called upon *to subordinate its sovereignty to the sovereignty of any other power, but to law itself,* that is, *to those rules of the game which we properly call "international law."* This is a distinction which may be difficult for the general public to appreciate, especially in view of the fact that during war our nation, like others, stresses its national sovereignty. To be sure, certain leaders of thought are now advocating a postwar alliance at least between England and America, as only the benighted still believe that a nation can by its own strength preserve its sovereignty. But alliances which recognize no sovereign international law are still only gangs without the law.

Jean Bodin is credited with giving the first clear formulation of sovereignty, which he defined as "the supreme power over citizens and subjects, unrestrained by the laws." But the sovereign is not exempt from all laws. "If we should define sovereignty as a power *legibus omnibus soluta,* no prince could be found to have sovereign rights; for all are bound by divine law and the law of nature and also by that common law of nations which embodies principles distinct from these." [6] The claim of any nation to absolute sovereignty is mythical and can be maintained only by the jungle law that might makes right.

In order to establish justice we must determine the seat of sovereignty. There must be some voice which has the last word. In America that final word of authority is spoken by the people. Our highest executive officer, the president, is commander in chief of our armed forces and in time of war is granted almost dictatorial powers. He salutes no other human being, but there is one thing which he does salute— the flag, the symbol of the sovereign will of the people.

Yet this so-called sovereign people, when it inaugurates a president, requires him to take an oath, or affirmation, symbolizing his recognition of divine sanction and authority. And when our national legislative bodies convene, their sessions are opened with prayer invoking the wisdom and aid of a divine Lawmaker. Moreover, our Constitution explicitly sets aside certain areas of freedom, such as that of conscience, in which the citizen is responsible directly to God alone. Thus implicitly and explicitly we recognize that this "government of the people, by the people, for the people" is also "this nation under God."

THE REALM OF UNWRITTEN LAW

The relations of men are too subtle to be regulated entirely by statute law. Justice requires a more illumined imagination,

[6] *De Republica,* p. 132.

a more sensitive conscience, and higher sanctions than laws and courts can approximate.

Lord Moulton, the eminent British jurist, reminds us that the area of human conduct can be divided into three zones. In one zone are those actions which can be regulated by statute law, such as real-estate transactions, rates of wages, criminal procedures, and the countless concrete actions on which legislatures pass laws by the tome and the ton. In a second zone are those attitudes which should be beyond the reach of law, such as freedom of conscience and freedom of thought. But in between these two zones is a third region of conduct which Lord Moulton calls the "domain of Obedience to the Unenforceable." It includes all those actions which we do when there is no one but ourselves to make us do them, all those restraints which we observe when there is no law or social control to hold us back.[7]

This realm of unwritten law, where men obey the unenforceable, may be observed in the home. In the business world, hours and wages are regulated by statute law. But there is no wages-and-hours schedule in the labors of family devotion. There is no ceiling to the cost of service a mother will pay for a sick child. If death breaks up a home and the property adjustments are thrown into court, there are laws which apportion the share of a widow or child. But while the home is a going institution it is run by unwritten laws. When children are little, they pull no oar in the boat. They are only passengers, a precious cargo to be sure, but very exacting. Yet parents keep no ledger account of their children's cost in expectation of future repayment. When parents become aged and infirm, they in turn are passengers to be carried. But dutiful sons and daughters do not desert helpless fathers and

[7] "Law and Manners," *Atlantic Monthly,* July, 1942, p. 31.

mothers. When the teamwork of husband and wife is broken by illness, the well partner carries the sick one. No laws are devised to cover all such contingencies, beyond that general vow taken at the marriage altar "for better, for worse, . . . in sickness and in health."

Or this realm of unwritten law may be seen in those emergencies where the highest impulses of man are revealed. Take the incident cited by Lord Moulton. Thirty years ago when the "Titanic" struck an iceberg and rapidly went to her watery grave, the passengers on that great liner observed the rule "Ladies first." No written law required the men to stand back while the women took to the lifeboats. No force compelled such conduct. But by the unwritten law of chivalry the gentlemen remained gentlemen, even to the edge of death.

And this obedience to the unenforceable is essential to freedom as well as to justice. Unless such obedience is inculcated, the lust for lawmaking, which is the trend of governments today, will spread until more and more areas of conduct come under the deadening blight of regulation and regimentation. If we would keep free from the encroaching overlordship of government, we must hold the self-control of our conduct as a sacred trust. Furthermore, a man is not made good by statute law. Law may force him to pay his income tax, but it cannot make him charitable. There is no goose-stepping goodness. Virtue, to be virtuous, must be born of free choice. Therefore unless we can live up to the unwritten laws of the free and the good life, we shall live down to the level of mental slavery and moral mediocrity.

At this point high religion plays an important role. It gives those sanctions which serve to keep a man obedient to the unenforceable. It strengthens and sensitizes a man's sense of honor—that sense of honor which keeps a husband loyal to his marriage vows, that holds a policeman to his post of dangerous duty, that sends a fireman into a burning building, that makes officers the last to leave a sinking ship. This sense of honor, noble and potent as it is, must be safeguarded and supplemented if men are to enjoy the free, good life. The medieval knights prided themselves on their honor and chivalry in dealing with the ladies of the nobility, but they had little compunction about defiling the daughters of the peasants. The sense of honor in Tokyo today is certainly different from the sense of honor as taught in London or Washington. Honor may be a most perverted thing when nurtured on a Nordic myth. The trouble with the sense of honor is that it so easily becomes narrowed into the code of a particular class or nation. One of the most difficult, even baffling, phases of building a just and durable peace after this war will be to find common ground where the diverse ideas of honor can secure respect for common law.

When the spirit of Christ gets into the atmosphere of a culture, it lifts codes of honor out of the narrow confines of class or nation or race. It makes a man want to do that which is "honorable among all men." It makes him desire to be honorable enough not only to do his duty as he sees it but to find out what his duty is, not only to tell the facts as he hears them but also to find out the facts before he tells them, not only to stand by his word but also to make his word worth standing by. If justice is to be established, it will require something more inclusive and more creative than statute laws and gentlemanly codes of honor. That something more is the spirit of Christ.

insure domestic Tranquility

THE INTEGRATED INDIVIDUAL

The insurance of domestic tranquillity must start with the integration of the individual. The disorganized person in our present sorely beset society is as threatening to others' welfare as is a rudderless ship in a convoy surrounded by submarines with a storm raging.

The problem of integration is not so much one of divided, but of subdivided, personality. A boy appears to be one personality in his home, another in his gang, another in his Sunday-school class. In his various relationships he may use different vocabularies and manifest different behaviors, because he discovers that recognition and response from others are solicited by different types of conduct. According to William James, a man has "as many different selves as there are distinct groups of persons about whose opinion he cares." And in keeping up these external social fronts, he so often develops basic divisions between the inner self and the outer selves. A person uses up his energy in conserving an inner emptiness under a shell of pretense. He strains to keep up a bold front which will hide his weak reserves. He struggles to maintain a reputation at variance with his true character. This inner tension, this strain of pretense, saps his moral strength and destroys the sincerity essential to individual integration and social security.

How is one to develop that inner core of consistency which

is the mark of the mature person and the making of a good member of society? At once we think of Shakespeare's counsel:

> To thine own self be true,
> And it must follow, as the night the day,
> Thou canst not then be false to any man.

But suppose that advice, given by Polonius to young Laertes, had been spoken to Hamlet himself. Would the distraught and frantic Hamlet have understood what it meant to be true to himself? No. Man needs not only to be told to be true to himself but also to be shown what his true self is. And it is this double service which the spirit of Christ renders to personality. Christ reveals to a man his potentialities. He bids us judge ourselves not by what we have or by what we are but by what we can become. He disturbs us with dreams of our higher selves. He keeps the prodigal from remaining content in the far country of low desires. He shows us that we cannot realize the fullness of life on the level of the physical. When we abide in his words and let his words abide in us, our tastes and tendencies are so lifted that the tension between our higher and lower natures is resolved; and over the life at one with his, there steal "the peace of God which passeth all understanding," and that delicious sense of well-being which the Bible calls blessedness.

The soul for its unity needs a center of reference outside and above itself. Christ offers himself as that center and claims the sovereign loyalty which holds in line the soul's hierarchy of values. Yet while he fixes the center of a life's loyalty, he enlarges the circumference of its living. He makes his followers alive and alert to more points of social content. He lengthens the gamut of human interests and yet restrains those childish instincts which would pound on all the keys of satisfaction at once and thus miss the harmony of happiness. By co-ordinating man's chaotic impulses he leads to that luminous living which comes through singleness of eye and that fullness which comes through simplicity.

The integration of personality requires also a unifying purpose. Yonder is a youth whose life is at odds and ends. He has been going around in circles and tangling himself in knots. He has been wasting his energies in wayward exploits and wasting his father's money in foolish extravagance. Then he is gripped by a great love or a consuming purpose. And we see him straighten out as does a coiled and twisted garden hose when a strong current of water is turned on. We see his vagrant impulses unite to give him force and effectiveness. We say that he has found himself.

But not every purpose which gives a person driving power imparts a lasting unity to his life. A man may find himself in his work and for a time go driving ahead under full steam and then at the end discover, as did Charles Darwin, that he had allowed some of his talents to atrophy. And how common is the case of the man who disintegrates rapidly after his retirement from business. War undoubtedly gives a temporary purposefulness to multitudes. Women of leisure find a satisfaction of soul in turning from a cloying idleness to the arduous tasks of war work. An electric energy galvanizes listless spirits into zestful activity. But one of the tragedies of war is that it leaves a trail of burned-out hopes and deflated ideals. The love of another person can give a glowing and a driving purpose to life, but human love in itself is not enough to keep one going when death takes away one's life partner. Various are the purposes which can set a life spinning like a top, but they run down and life topples over.

At this point Christ supplements and supersedes all other unifying purposes. Unto a life truly committed to him Christ imparts a sense of divine mission. And a sense of mission is something more consuming and continuous than the aims and objectives which move a life from point to point. Eventually we have to retire from our business or profession, our "life work," but we never have to retire from a life mission in the Christian sense. Eventually death separates us from the earthly comradeship of our loved ones, but "who shall separate us from the love of Christ? shall tribulation, or distress, or persecution, or famine, or nakedness, or peril, or sword?" Nay, for "in all these things we are more than conquerors through him that loved us."

A life is left at loose ends if it has only temporary and transient purposes. These must be tied by a philosophy of life into purposes and plans which transcend our individual welfare and outrun our individual existence. Gilbert Murray of Oxford, in giving his views on the re-education of German youth, tells this incident: "A friend of mine once took a German—an exiled and persecuted German—to a lecture at the London School of Economics on the principles of democracy. My friend thought it a fine lecture, but the German broke out in indignation against the English and American views of life which think always of 'the happiness of the greatest number,' of the 'welfare of the individual,' of amusement and comfort, of 'having a good time,' as if such things as those were the true end of life. What the German demanded was some high and heroic aim to which the individual could devote himself, whatever it might involve of toil and suffering. It is a dangerous aim when misdirected, but one which must at least be understood by anyone who

VERNON REGIONAL
JUNIOR COLLEGE LIBRARY

hopes to co-operate with Germans in the re-education of Germany." [1]

Yes, and we would add that the German refugee's viewpoint merits consideration by those who would shape the future education of our free countries. To be sure, the desire of the individual for some high heroic aim to which he can submit himself has been misdirected and prostituted by dictators. But the principle is valid and basic. He that would find his life must lose it in some cause larger than himself. Christ came to enlist men in such causes. "He that loseth his life for my sake shall find it." But our democratic way of life, which boasts itself the political embodiment of Christian principles, has diverted its emphasis from self-commitment to self-enrichment, forgetting that the individual best gets what belongs to him when he has a sense of belonging. Truly, institutions are made for man and not man for the institutions, whether they be the Sabbath, the family, the church, or the state. Nevertheless, man must have a sense of belonging to these institutions if he is to receive richly what they are designed to give. And we of the democracies, with our emphasis on rights rather than on responsibilities, have trained our citizens to be concerned with what the group can do for them rather than with what they can do for the group.

Unless we of the free countries can find ourselves by losing ourselves in high heroic purposes, future Hitlers and future "isms" will arise to prostitute man's craving for completion. We are designed to be spans in the bridge of purposes stretching across the generations. We have a sense of the eternal significance which cannot be satisfied with personal possessions or even with planned public economies.

[1] *New York Times,* May 16, 1943.

In his *Three Cities* Sholem Asch portrayed the puzzlement
of a young recruit during early days of the Russian revolution. The youth was swept along by the enthusiasm of his
communist colleagues. But he kept asking what they believed about God and immortality and personal destiny. In
their eagerness for the new social order they were impatient
with such old-fashioned questions. To them it seemed sufficient to set up a world of equal rights. But to him the ends
seemed too shallow and short to justify the ruthless means
employed to attain them. The abandonment of religious
hopes and sanctions in their revolutionary zeal reminded the
serious young recruit of the woman who emptied the bed
of its feathers and then tried to recover them one by one.
To such a figure the critic might reply that one trouble with
traditional religion has been that it serves as a bed on which
men sleep amid the social inequities of the present world,
and therefore to empty it of its softness is a service to man.
But the remedy for softening religious otherworldliness does
not lie in an economic revolution or in a succession of five-
year plans. The re-entrance of the church on the Russian stage
under official sanction is explained as the turning to God
"for guidance, help, and comfort in their sorrow and agony." [2]

Admittedly conventional Christianity has been softening.
Our professedly Christian democracies have tended to develop the spirit of getting rather than giving, and churches
have catered to their members rather than challenged them.
The result has been to disintegrate the individual rather than
to unify. When, therefore, we present Christ as the one able
to integrate personality, we are calling for a redirection of
trends in Christian culture. We are summoning ourselves

[2] Archbishop of York, as reported in the *New York Times,* October 12,
1943.

to a search for the longer clues to life's larger meaning. We are challenging the churches to a religious education which furnishes a reason for the faith that is in us and to a social program which summons into use the power that is beyond us.

WORK

We go on to look at certain points of tension where domestic tranquillity is now most disturbed. One of these is in the realm of work.

Work is essential to personal integration and domestic tranquillity. Without something to work on, human energies turn in on themselves with destructive force. Deprived of work, people exhaust themselves like caged animals beating against the bars. To find one's work is to find a place in the world. It gives one courage. It is an anodyne to grief. It is a link with other comrades.

Yet work, which is so essential to making a life, is commonly discussed as if it were an unpleasant requirement for making a living. We talk of it in terms of hours and wages —hours to be shortened if possible, wages to be increased if possible. Many a parent says: "I am going to give my children an education so that they will not have to work as hard as I have worked." If one were to judge from the conversation of the street, he would conclude that work is a more or less painful prelude to the enjoyment of living.

This attitude is not necessarily a sign that men are being made soft and lazy. It is not merely the spirit of work which needs to be cultivated; it is the status of work which is to be rehabilitated. We must reintegrate work with our other cultural activities. We must recover for work its educational and spiritual significance. We should so order work that children can find their happy place in it and the elderly may not be deprived of it. Modern science and industrialization have developed a cruel paradox. With our improved medical skill we have lengthened man's productive years, but with our improved machines we have shortened his period of employability. Work should not be regarded as something which starts at 8:00 A.M. and ends at 5:00 P.M., nor as something which begins at eighteen and ends at sixty-five. Work is a God-given functional activity by which men live. And we must habituate ourselves to viewing work in its spiritual perspective as a basis to its economic aspects.

If work is to make for individual and social tranquillity, it must be inspired by a satisfying incentive. Vital human effort cannot be sustained without the feeling that the work being done is worth while. The Carpenter of Nazareth recognized the factor of reward in stimulating endeavor. There is a Christian profit motive. But we have de-Christianized it by making it too exclusively economic, and we have debased work by treating this money-making profit motive as its mainspring. The Archbishop of Canterbury views the matter in Christian perspective when he says: "The profit motive is not simply evil. It can have its own right place. But that is not the first place, and the harm in the predominance of the profit motive is not merely that it is an expression of selfishness whether the form it takes is concerned with dividends or wages, but that to put this first may lead to an ordering of economic life which in fact is damaging to the general interest." [3]

Recognizing that the predominance of the profit motive creates a bad ordering of economic life, may we not also reverse the Archbishop's sequence and say that the ordering

[3] Address at meeting of Industrial Christian Fellowship in Albert Hall, London, as reported in the *New York Times,* September 27, 1942.

of the economic life leads to overemphasis of the profit motive? Longfellow's village blacksmith, who

> Each morning, sees some task begun,
> Each evening sees it close,

has the satisfaction of viewing his handiwork in such completeness as to feel it to be his own. Thus feeling the spur of creativity and the pride of achievement, he is not dependent on financial profit for his reward. But the village blacksmith is vanishing before the advancing factory system. And as for the factory worker who merely drives rivets into frames on a moving production line, where is his creative motive? Where is the satisfaction of his artistic urge? In the temporary emotionalism of war he may feel a patriotic fervor and may share pride in the "E" awarded by the government to his company, but ordinarily he is left looking to his pay envelope for his reward. The artist in his studio, the chemist in his laboratory, the preacher in his pulpit—all have the incentive of creating and the reward of social recognition; but these lures are lacking to those who are mere "hands," known to their executives by number rather than name, and wholly unknown to their absentee employers. When work becomes so depersonalized, it is little wonder that the worker's eye is single to the profit motive.

Moreover, not only is work thus monetized by being depersonalized, but we live in a society which more and more tends to rate men by what they spend rather than by what they produce. On the farm in the days of my boyhood, farmers were measured by the quality of their crops and the efficiency of their farm management, not by the size of their houses and the models of their cars. But now in our city environments we are inclined to rate people by the expensiveness and location of their residences, the number of their servants, the general scale of their living. With men's work lost in the anonymity of depersonalized corporations, we form our social circles, scarcely asking what our associates do or produce provided they live and spend on our level. As long as we rate men socially by what they spend rather than by what they produce, we sharpen that spirit of greed which grabs for the largest possible income with the least possible service.

Henry Ford is reported as saying, "All men want is to be told what to do and get paid for doing it." [4] That certainly was not all Mr. Ford himself wanted. And when exceptional and able men impute such motives to the masses of workers, they show a lack of understanding which widens the chasms of distrust. Nazi youth may want nothing more than to be told what to do, but even Hitler was shrewd enough to see that he must stir his followers by some motive other than personal pay. He aroused their fervor by his frenzied appeals for the fatherland. Our American workers have not been trained in the Nazi tradition of regimentation, and certainly they are not so mercenary as to be more intent on the profit motive than are the hordes of Hitler.

Some years ago a highly regarded social investigator, after long association with factory workers, came to the conclusion that man's mainspring motive is to feel himself a person among other persons. If men could be given the feeling that they count as persons in the community of labor and not as hands in a factory, that they count as persons in the community of living regardless of the money they receive and spend, then their eyes would cease to be strained on the profit motive. What chiefly disturbs men's peace of mind and our

[4] *Time,* March 17, 1941, p. 19.

nation's domestic tranquillity is not that some men receive more income than others but that the possession of more money makes such a difference in their relationships. Inequality of income does not need to make such a marked disparity between people, and in some communities it does not do so. Where contacts are sufficiently close and personal, character and ability count rather than money. The five-talent man and the one-talent man live congenially and contentedly side by side, because each appraises and respects the other for what he is rather than for what he has.

If we are to lessen the disturbing and pernicious effects of the profit motive, we must create a social atmosphere in which men find a personal standing more independent of financial position. Money talks as long as people listen to it, and men turn deaf ears to the voice of Midas only if their interest is aroused elsewhere. To arouse that interest many factors must conspire: those who work in mass production must be given some outlet for personal creativity, either within the factory or after hours; persons will have to be rated more by the quality of their lives than by the scale of their living; the church must cease to measure ministers by salary and congregations by wealth—in short, all departments of culture must join in dethroning the profit motive from its ruling position.

It is shortsighted to put the burden of blame on organized labor for its imputed greed or to think the profit motive can be restrained by abolishing the capitalistic system. "What is needed is a change of mind and heart rather than a change of system. We do not want to get rid of our country's traditional national ideals; we want to take them seriously and live up to them. We do not want to get rid of the system of free enterprise and capitalism; we want to take it seriously—

to live up to its basic principles where they are helpful, to
improve them where necessary. . . . The system did not break
down of its own defects. It broke down because of the moral
defects of all of us, the spiritual thinness of our Western life,
which permitted the system first to become an end in itself
and then to betray even its own rules in the interest of immediate greed." [5]

To insure domestic tranquillity we must give immediate
attention to the present tensions as well as to the motives of
work. Labor and management have drawn up a truce during
the war emergency, but beware of what may follow unless
better bases of understanding are reached. Both sides seem
to be living on the defensive, expecting attack. The well-to-do
seem almost more haunted by fears than are the poor. Mentally barricaded behind its fears and class prejudices, each side
lives more and more to itself. The friendly contacts of a
former era are lacking.

On the farm and in the small factories of earlier days, employer and employee were personally acquainted and shared
each other's interests; but men who work in large units and
live in cities are deprived of such contacts. The changed skyline of New York or any other large city is symbolic of this
changed status. A view of old New York reveals a low,
almost level, line of buildings, the very evenness of the skyline symbolizing the comparative social equality of the inhabitants. Shop owners and clerks walked the same streets,
sent their children ordinarily to the same district school, went
to the same church. Today the skyline of Manhattan or Chi-
cago is broken by skyscrapers which rise to dizzying height
while alongside are yawning chasms to provide light and air
for the lofty structures, the unevenness symbolizing the in-

[5] Herbert Agar, *A Time for Greatness,* Little, Brown & Co., 1942, p. 172.

equalities and separateness now existing. Riding separately in public and private conveyances, educated separately in public and private schools, worshiping separately, if at all, in class-conscious churches, the employee and the employer now lack the friendly contacts which were one of the original and fruitful characteristics of the American tradition. Taxes and other forms of socialization may reduce the inequalities, but they will not restore the neighborliness.

Only a revived sense of community can redirect the present trend toward industrial feudalism back toward friendliness. The five-talent and the one-talent individuals must have sufficient points of contact to generate mutual understanding and respect. They can and must break through their separate compartments of living and get the feeling of belonging to the same community. Toward this end city planning can contribute by constructing inexpensive but good housing near enough for the occupants to share the same neighborhood schools and churches. The rich may try to seek exclusiveness by building elsewhere, but they will not continue to run away from the bonds of fellow-citizenship if there is developed a social spirit which stamps such escape with the stigma now placed on those who refuse to buy victory bonds in time of war. Community spirit can be raised to the level of patriotism in time of peace as in war. Management can cultivate the personal acquaintance, the personal confidence, and also the counsel of labor. Some farsighted business leaders are willing to welcome the representatives of labor on their boards of directors.

Enlightened self-interest is calling for a new sense of community feeling and co-operation. Listen to this statement from the president of the United States Chamber of Commerce: "Only by realizing that we cannot be prosperous unless the whole economy prospers are we (in business) able to fill our mission in a world eager for the new scales of comfort, convenience and plenty which business in its youth and vigor will provide. The new capitalism, from which there can be no retreat, is predicated upon the sound conviction that the greatest good for business comes from what is best for the greatest number. And to that end it is learning to work with labor, the farmer and government for an America that will be good for us all." [6]

Yet the dissolving of the present tensions calls for a spirit deeper than enlightened self-interest. Co-operation and charity prompted by expediency are not enough. We must advance from the expediency of fellowship to the experience of it. The money labels must be removed from our subconscious minds as well as from our success patterns. The dignity of manual labor must be felt. Good craftsmen should be accorded a social recognition akin to that received by the banker or factory owner. The church must prove itself a conciliator. Instead of denouncing labor czars from the pulpit on the avenue and thus lending support to organized labor's contention that it is the tool of the well-to-do, let the church try to secure the attendance and gain the confidence of union members and leaders. Let us bring the brotherhood which was in Christ down to earth by consecrating all our cultural agencies to the task.

Does all this seem a counsel of perfection? Here, as elsewhere, we must approach the ideal by way of intermediate steps. There are paths in the wilderness pointing toward this community of spirit. Our task is to make these into highways of real advance. Already the church has commissions studying

[6] Eric A. Johnston, " 'An End to Reaction'—A Charter for Business," *New York Times Magazine.* August 22, 1943.

labor relations. Local churches are making attempts to get the viewpoint of organized labor. Communities are organizing "town meetings" where economic questions are frankly discussed and, better yet, are promoting co-operative enterprises in which class distinctions are often forgotten. Old Eastern universities like Harvard are democratizing their student bodies by means of scholarships open to all on a competitive basis, and family distinctions have a way of fading in these campus comradeships. The leaven of democracy may be seen at work in the associations formed by those daughters of the rich who increasingly are entering the fields of employment. And certainly war scrambles some of the social distinctions. Boys on the same bomber form a brotherhood of bravery independent of family background. Such are some of the trails which can be widened into highways of real brotherhood.

Here, as in the pursuit of our objectives, it is a case of "we the people." The creation of a spirit or atmosphere is the cumulative radiation of individual influence. Each one of us has daily some opportunity to make for domestic tranquillity as against turmoil. In this sphere of work we are "laborers together with God," who is "able to do exceeding abundantly above all that we ask or think, according to the power that worketh in us."

RECREATION

Play, like work, is essential to individual integration and social tranquillity. Play reveals character. If you wish to know the quality of a person, watch him in his off hours, when he is free to do what he likes to do. Play recreates as well as reveals—or it should. But so much that is popularly called recreation does not recreate. America is in as much danger of being undone through the misuse of her leisure as through the mismanagement of her labor.

This constructive direction of recreation will challenge us immediately after the war. The memory of what happened after Versailles stirs us with anxiety for the future. The last war was followed by what has been called the "jazz age." We speeded life up to such a tempo during the war that we could not slow down into simple, wholesome pleasures when the excitement was over. So we organized dance marathons, million-dollar prize fights, "jitterbug contests," and various bizarre, neurotic, and erotic forms of entertainment too numerous to mention. As a result, our nerves went ragged and our morals ran loose. In the words of Hendrik van Loon, the experience was like taking a joy ride with a cave man in a Chevrolet. We dashed down the broad and easy highway of the spacious twenties like racing motorists on the way to bigger and better business, more exciting and exotic thrills. Then came the financial crash of 1929 to form a bottleneck in the road. Unchastened and undisciplined, we commenced honking for the right of way; and now the honking 1930's have deteriorated into the shooting 1940's.

From soldiers to playboys, then back to soldiering again—such has been the swing of history's pendulum. When the disciplines of war are relaxed, we let ourselves go until we drift into danger again. Shall we continue this vicious circle?

An exiled German educator, Dr. Reinhold Schairer, speaking from personal observation, says: "Recreation well directed can change the habits and character of men. Through misuse of the recreational activities, Japan and Germany have transformed their youth into perfect tools of destruction. We must do the opposite." [7]

[7] *New York Times*, September 30, 1942.

If recreation is to serve as a constructive and tranquilizing force, it must find more sources in simple things. The multiplication of material and mechanical resources has lessened our inner resourcefulness. It is easier to sit down and be entertained by a moving picture than to use our own imaginations in making the characters of a book come to life. It is less effort to turn on the radio than to exercise our powers of conversation. And when it is so easy to tune in on a dance orchestra, we are less likely to cultivate the birds outside our windows. In the accelerated tempo of our time, we rush through our working hours and then hurry to some place of amusement where others work to entertain us. The resulting tendency of such an attitude is the atrophy of our inner initiating faculties of enjoyment, such as imagination and meditation. The wealth of sensations made possible by radio and screen can make for richer cultural interests if we use care to be selective and effort to be imaginative and time to be meditative. These are the necessities we now neglect.

Furthermore, if we use our leisure in ways that cost least mental energy and imagination, we drain off our inner urges on the lower levels of satisfaction. Thus the sex instinct is expended on the low level of lust and does not fulfill its God-given function of replenishing the springs of creative art.

Then, too, dependence on external sources of recreation makes for artificiality and extravagance. The current cost of one evening's pleasure in a large city would have paid for grandfather's honeymoon. The strain of keeping up with the crowd spoils the enjoyment of social fellowship and the domestic tranquillity of the home. Because the home is caught in this cult of crowd comparisons, young people may postpone marriage until they think themselves financially able to keep up with their "set," or young husbands and wives may keep their respective jobs and delay child rearing until they think they can afford it. The ill effects of both postponements need not be dwelt on here. Unless we find the way back to the simple noncompetitive sources of recreation, we are headed for disaster.

After the last war Louis Bromfield produced a panel of books depicting the efforts of restless America to find some new frontiers. Since his young men could no longer "go west and grow up with the country," they went east and went down with the city. Recently Mr. Bromfield himself has been developing a farm in Ohio, and apparently finding immense satisfaction. May it be that in this author's experience is to be seen a symbol of hope? Has the search for artificial thrills sufficiently disillusioned us to turn us toward the simple life? Let us not only hope, but let us also strive to make it so. Let us rediscover and conserve our natural resources for enjoyment. When we have the initiative and imagination to find recreation in the simple God-owned things of nature, we become independent of the curse of crowd comparisons. In our enjoyments we do not have to keep up with anyone else or take away from anyone else. The more beauty we cultivate, the more we make available for others. In the realm of noncompetitive, self-creating recreation, there are no "ceilings" to restrict us by social compulsion. The sky is the limit.

If we are to meet the challenge of making recreation constructive, we need to educate our cultural tastes. Modern education and means of communication have widened rather than deepened cultural interests. The youth of today have a wider acquaintance with painting and music than had those of an earlier generation, but on the whole their tastes are unorganized and superficial. The contemporary attitude recalls the old proverb: "The slothful man roasteth not that which he took in hunting: but the substance of a diligent man is precious." We are sensation hunters, novelty seekers. We are avid for what we call life. But, like the slothful hunter, we find it so much more interesting to hunt than to prepare our catch to be the food of our minds and spirits. Therefore we collect so much more than we use, and we waste such a wealth of possible enjoyment. Libraries contain collections of rare books, but those who appreciate them are quite as rare. Art museums are visited by a few thousands, while Hollywood's films draw their daily millions. We have more good tastes, but not necessarily more good taste. We have more cultural channels of recreation, but they are shallower.

However, serious and constructive efforts at educating our cultural tastes are under way. Our public schools are making marked advances in the democratization of genuinely good art and music. It is heartening to note the rising quality of programs rendered by high school orchestras and choruses during the last decade. Another movement giving much promise is the circulation of art reproductions through the schools and colleges of our country, bringing the boy in Nebraska or Texas face to face with the classic creations of the world's greatest painters and sculptors. Cities fortunate enough to have art museums are fostering an acquaintance with them on the part of school children. The radio, despite the defects of some of its programs, is doing immeasurable service to public taste by making symphonies and operas available to the millions.

And certain communities are beginning to take adult education seriously. Maplewood, New Jersey, to cite only one instance, had before the war some four thousand citizens enrolled in weekly courses taught by faculty members of Princeton, Columbia, New York University, and other leading schools. This program was planned and carried out with the same balance and care as that given to university courses. When a community thus changes the mental diet of its members from a haphazard gorging of radio and press offerings into a well-organized program of adult education, it is insuring the vitamins which make for moral and spiritual health.

In this organization and education of cultural tastes, the key agencies are the old trinity: the home, the school, and the church—homes in which parents study to keep abreast of the growing interests of the children, homes which give more intelligent attention to the art within and the gardens without, which plan diversions so that parents do more things with their children and fewer things for them; schools which seek to educate parents as well as pupils, which consider education for leisure as important as technical training for work, which try to impart an interest in cultural arts and studies sufficient to keep the graduates pursuing them in later years; churches which recognize that beauty and truth belong with goodness, which regard aids to wholesome diversion as more effective than prohibitions of bad amusements, which seriously undertake to pervade the atmosphere of their members' whole cultural life with the joyous creativity of the Christ spirit.

If we meet this challenge of constructive recreation, we shall see a flowering of the fine arts such as our best utilitarian period never dreamed. Franz Werfel makes two of his characters in *The Song of Bernadette* hold a conversation which may irritate some of our sensitivities but should also illumine our thinking. Lafite, the agnostic aesthete, remarks: "In ages when the Church was a great Church the highest art was her handmaiden. For nothing human is holier than that high beauty which is found incarnate in high art. I cannot consider a Church as partaking of holiness when it is faithless to beauty either because it shares the taste of these cave-dwellers or is unwilling to offend it." To this, Estrade, another intellectual, answers: "Suppose we reverse your saying, dear friend. When art was high art, the Church stood at its side. . . ." [8]

The church, we believe, is reawakening to the holiness of beauty. The American church is not content to concentrate that beauty in shrines of worship while surrounding homes are left in drabness and poverty. We want beauty to be a pervasive thing, led by religious influence, for it is in religion that high art has found its richest sources of inspiration. And above all we want this cultivation of beauty to be sincere. The late Ralph Adams Cram was wont to say that a church structure to be genuinely Christian should get better the farther in you go. The church thus symbolizes the Christlike life, which it is designed to develop. Sincerity gives beauty to simplicity, which is the direction to be sought by our modern Babylon before our towers fall through the weight of their extravagance and the strain of their pretense.

And this constructive channeling of our recreation toward beauty will exert a tranquilizing and universalizing influence beyond measure. Art begets a sense of brotherhood beyond class, race, and national lines. In the spring of 1927, on the occasion of the centenary of Beethoven's death, a series of concerts lasting seven days was given in Tokyo before crowded and enthusiastic audiences. The present bonds between Japan and Germany were not wholly forged by military cliques. Some ties were woven by the German musicians who have been guiding the teaching of the best classical music in

[8] The Viking Press, 1942, pp. 533-34.

Japanese schools. "Music hath charms to soothe the savage breast," and those charms will be needed for the calming process to follow the brutality of this war. They must be cultivated with a speed and range never approached before. Both domestic tranquillity and world brotherhood depend as much on cultural exchange as on trade treaties and international agreements. All are creators of the atmosphere in which peace is to live and move and have its being.

OUR STRANGLING ALLIANCES

In his *Loyalties* John Galsworthy pictures the meshwork of entangling alliances in which we live and work and play. An English army officer steals from a wealthy Jew who is being entertained at the same house party. He takes the money to purchase the silence of an Italian girl with whom he has been too intimate. Then the entangling alliances begin to tighten their stranglehold. The Jew, bitter at being blackballed at a London club, brings suit against the army captain. The army crowd, motivated by class and racial loyalties, stand by the captain. The girl's father, in loyalty to his family, tries to hush the matter up. The captain's wife, through her family loyalty, stands by her husband. Certain attorneys refuse to take the case, out of loyalty to the standards of their profession. Thus the roots of loyalty become so snarled that, as one of those involved said, "crisscross, we cut each other's throats with the best of motives."

While loyalty is one of the best motives, the results here were far from even second-best. In our increasingly inter-meshed life, domestic tranquillity demands a vine dresser who keeps the roots of loyalty from choking one another and prevents the branches of growing interests from shutting others out of a place in the sun. And speaking in no sectarian but in a broadly catholic sense, we believe that Christ is the one who can keep the garden of social living from becoming a jungle of conflicting loyalties.

The spirit of Christ starts this gardening work in the intimate loyalties of what we call our "domestic circles." Christ would purge from the family that spirit of possessiveness which mars the luster of marriage. His spirit has helped to lift woman toward an equal status of rights and education. In a Christian household the wife is no longer the child-bearing property of her husband but his mental and social equal. In the relations of the home Christ imparts the spirit of charitableness which is courteously considerate of differences and forgiving toward shortcomings. Intimate personal love is not self-sustaining in isolation. For its own preservation love requires the sharing of common interests, common goals, a common faith. This sharing is supplied by Christ, for his presence enlarges the outlooks and widens the sympathies.

Then, using the family as his pattern, Christ runs the roots of loyalty out into the surrounding social areas. To him God is a father, all men are brothers, and therefore society is the family of God. Jesus was realistic enough not to expect human nature to feel the same intimate affection towards strangers as towards members of the same household. The Gospels use a more intimate word to describe the relations between parent and child than to express the attitude enjoined toward neighbors and enemies. This is a distinction which should be borne in mind. So much talk about loving neighbors and enemies falls on deaf ears because it sounds too sentimentally impossible. To think that we can feel the same love toward a stranger as toward a twin brother seems as far beyond human nature as the mathematical theories of Einstein are beyond the use of the paperhanger. In fact it is difficult to find the English word which adequately expresses the social attitude called for by Christ. Jerome, in taking the Greek into the Latin, used *caritas,* which has come down to us as "charity;" but it has been professionalized almost as badly as the word "love" has been sentimentalized. Careful Christian writers now use the Greek word *agape.* Perhaps the nearest approach to its meaning is good will that is active and passionate enough to become redemptive love.

Christ expects his followers to have not a passive but a passionate good will. Our own self-respect is the yardstick by which we are to measure our regard for others. We are to consider the rights of others as fully as our own. We are not to force our views on them any more than we allow them to thrust their views on us. We shall not try to use them any further than we wish them to use us.

The spirit of Christ makes a man magnanimous, and magnanimity is an expansiveness of soul which gives winsomeness to other virtues. It is a certain greatness of nature which lifts a person above petty insults and little grudges. The magnanimous man feels that he is below himself when he is not above an injury. He puts a good interpretation on the motives of others. He rejoices in the success of his rivals. Magnanimity, according to Hazlitt, is the rarest of our virtues, for there are a hundred persons of merit to one who willingly acknowledges merit in others.

Starting in such a magnanimous spirit, Christian good will ripens in the pervading consciousness of God's fatherhood. The Christlike person loves because God first loved him, because God is love. This divine genesis of good will delivers it from the casualness and the casualties of merely human love. It generates a love which goes out to the just and the unjust, to friend and foe. "But I say unto you, Love your enemies, bless them that curse you, do good to them that hate you, and pray for them which despitefully use you, and persecute you; *that ye may be the children of your Father which is in heaven: for he maketh his sun to rise on the evil and on the good, and sendeth rain on the just and on the unjust.*"

Christ here uses on a large scale a principle which we see applied in family relationships. How does an older child learn to care for the newly born brother or sister who comes to share his playthings and eventually to divide his patrimony? By catching from the parents the love which they shower on the little one. Parental affection creates the atmosphere in which love between children flourishes. So in society at large, belief in God's fatherhood is the atmosphere in which brotherly love breathes and has its being if it is to survive "the whips and scorns of time."

Thus, beginning in the unchangeable good will of God and not in the flimsy and fluctuating feelings of human likableness, Christian love begets a brotherly view of one's fellow men. By doing good to others we come to see the good in others. If it is true that we come to hate those we wrong, it is equally true that we learn to love those we help. And if our helpfulness extends to one who has wronged us, we "heap coals of fire on his head" which not only burn him with shame for his wrongdoing but, if our good deed is done with true charitableness and humility, melt his resentment and also warm our own hearts toward him with a new sense of his inherent worth. They become a hearth fire at which both the forgiving and the forgiven are warmed. By acting as sons of God we come to realize and respect the dignity and worth of God's other sons.

And if the spirit of Christ is in our hearts, we see our fellow men as individuals and not in the mass—as persons, not as problems. Jesus did not talk about the problem of the foreigner, but he did tell the parable of a good Samaritan. He did not prate about "the problem of the underprivileged," but he did help his hearers to look at life through the eyes of poor widows and prodigal boys who were down and out. Jesus did not deliver appeals for such vague entities as "society" or "humanity." He saw the persons behind the statistics. This is a point often missed by modern reformers and humanitarians. In our day there are too many parlor socialists who are personal snobs, too many uplifters who wish to manufacture brotherhood in wholesale quantities but cannot bother with individual customers.

On the other hand, the Christ spirit would not have us be sentimentalists who salve our consciences by little acts of personal kindness. The fact that I played with a Negro lad in my boyhood and have kept in touch with him ever since, the fact that I have some very close friends belonging to the Roman Catholic faith and to the Jewish race—these are not enough to demonstrate my Christian brotherhood. I must be concerned to see that these racial and religious minorities have the same right I covet for myself.

To insure domestic tranquillity we must work with persons and principles rather than with problems and sentimentality. Much is said and written about "the problem of Harlem," mostly by persons who do little or nothing about it. "The problem of the Jew" is a favorite topic of private conversation and public discussion, but instead of fostering fellowship the discussion is likely to focus attention on race prejudice. At a meeting of a religious committee on racial minorities some few years ago, the question was raised as to publicizing certain incidents of anti-Jewish intolerance in Europe. A very intelligent Jewish leader opposed the featuring of the new facts on the ground that it would do more harm than good. His position is understandable. He did not desire the sufferings of his fellow Jews to serve merely as fuel for discussion which so often leaves a residue of added resentment.

To be sure, the racial, religious, and class tensions now disturbing our domestic tranquillity are very real problems which call for economic adjustments and political action. Every citizen should be studying and working to further these concrete solutions. The churches should have their national commissions and their local communities dealing with these issues. But basic to all this is the creation of an atmosphere in which these concrete reforms can function. We must see and cultivate the persons within, and above, the problems.

provide for the common defence

At a time when almost each new day brings forth some book on national defense, it is both unnecessary and impossible to attempt any broad survey of this subject in a brief chapter. Here as elsewhere we shall confine our discussion to certain phases of defense wherein the religious impact is most imperatively needed.

THE WATCH ON THE RAMPARTS

There are more watchmen on the ramparts of the world today than ever before. The reasons are obvious. Nations live closer together, and the conflicts of interest are more numerous and varied. Barricaded behind their national boundaries, people are living everywhere on the defensive. Distrust begets distrust and then poisons both possessors. As the shadows of suspicion thicken, more spokesmen find it profitable to play upon popular fears. Thus demagogues add to the hue and cry which drives the populace further into fear.

Another reason for the multiplication of watchmen is that events move so fast in these days. The faster we travel, the further ahead we have to look. We think that we cannot make our plans on the basis of what happened yesterday; we want to foresee what is going to happen tomorrow. It is not enough for us to be up to date; we wish to be up to tomorrow. Hence we have developed a new profession of seers who by radio and press columns interpret the news in an effort to see both behind and before the headlines.

It is not enough merely to multiply watchmen; much depends on the character of those who watch. Irresponsible watchmen are worse than none, for they deceive us with misinformation. Emotional watchmen are a menace, for they excite us without cause. Prejudiced watchmen are a peril, for they distort dangers and arouse our fears in wrong directions. And false prophets cry, "Peace, peace," when there is no peace. In a society honeycombed with fears and buzzing with propagandists, the cry "Watchman, what of the night?" should be supplemented with the cry "Night, what of the watchmen?"

The great Hebrew prophets were seers scanning the ramparts of Israel. In the nations of Christendom the church has provided watchmen for the ramparts. Religious leaders have served as the nerves of the commonwealth and the keepers of public conscience. In America the Colonial pulpits played a formative part in the securing of independence and in the development of the democratic principle. And now 129 potent churchmen have issued a "Declaration on World Peace," stating seven principles deemed basic to a just and durable peace. The publication of this declaration constitutes notice served on political leadership that it must submit its postwar program to the review and judgment of church and synagogue as interpreters of the moral law.

The relation of church and state will furnish one of the most acute issues during the next few decades. There has never been a uniformly accepted idea about the responsibilities of the Christian church to the state. But clear and commanding was the attitude of the first Christian before the legal tribunal when he boldly affirmed, "We must obey God rather than men." That mandate has never been revoked.

It does not follow that we cannot obey both God and the governmental rulers set over us. But we must know where the choice lies if we have to make one.

The separation of church and state is a doctrine dear to the American heart. We want no state church. We will tolerate no sectarian priorities, no secret ecclesiastical diplomacy. But we do believe in the sovereignty of God and in the right of his spokesmen to cultivate the conscience of the state.

The watchmen of God must remain on the ramparts of our republic in order to keep asserting the sovereignty of God. When three years ago the Archbishop of York proposed a basis of co-operation between Christians of all denominations, the first tenet of the creed suggested for the new unified movement was "God reigns." That is the fundamental tenet. From heaven he reigns—creator and upholder of the world. From the cross he reigns—making defeat itself the stuff of his triumph. And in the new "Declaration on World Peace," signed by the Jewish, Roman Catholic, and Protestant leaders, the first principle is: "The organization of a just peace depends upon practical recognition of the fact that not only individuals but nations, states and international society are subject to the sovereignty of God and to the moral law which comes from God."

Also it is imperative that the watchmen of God remain on the ramparts in order to safeguard the sanctity and worth of the individual. The church is not equipped to give expert advice in economic, political, and military spheres; but it can cry out whenever human values are being hurt, even though it cannot offer the concrete formula of cure. The church of the Great Physician can and must keep its finger on the pulse of the people. It can provide forums for the discussion of public policy and furnish incentives for governmental action.

The church should be the champion of human rights, insisting that individuals be treated as ends in themselves and preventing personality from being sacrificed on the altar of institutions.

Furthermore, the seers of God must remain on the ramparts in order to defend the values not yet established. "Base things of the world, and things which are despised, hath God chosen, yea, and things which are not, to bring to nought things that are." If we are to provide for the common defense, we must live on the growing edge of things, we must foresee and welcome the values which have not yet arrived. Any time-server can count the apples on the tree, but the God-server cultivates the trees in the apple. The prophet Jeremiah, in describing his call tells of a twofold vision. He saw a "seething pot; and the face thereof is toward the north." This was his figurative way of pointing out the peril of invasion—a thing which any news commentator could detect. But Jeremiah saw also "a rod of an almond tree," the budding signs of divine promise beneath the wintry bleakness of Israel's beleagured condition—a feature which the press columnist would not have the faith to see. Contrast this vision of Jeremiah—or the attitude of any of the great Hebrew prophets—with the following view of a popular present-day columnist: "Pessimist I may be, but nevertheless I insist that there is nothing in the past or current record of human nature to justify a belief or even a hope that mankind will step out of this war into a beautiful world of mutual love and trust and universal justice"—so far, so good, but read farther—"*or that such a state can ever be achieved.* What is my pattern of a postwar world, then? . . . It would be pretty much the same old world populated by the same old human race, but this time with the musket back over the fireplace where it belongs and not traded off for a set of embroidered mottoes." [1]

If this view is all that is to be seen from the ramparts, then they are hardly worth defending, certainly not at the cost of the blood and sweat and tears now being sacrificed. The watchmen of God do not expect this war to eventuate in a utopia; but they do reject the doctrine that man is a fighting animal and always will be, and that therefore wars are inevitable. The great Hebrew prophets and our Lord himself went to their deaths believing that men could be won to a brotherhood. To deny that is a dangerous heresy which damns all hope of progress.

THE RAMPARTS WE WATCH

The best defense of a nation is the sound morale of its citizenry. Improved mobile warfare renders Maginot lines obsolete. The planes and submarines of today will be scrapped tomorrow. The important factor in defense is not so much what we have in hand as what we can lay our hands on. It is the resources and resourcefulness of a people which best provide for the common defense.

Morale means healthy-mindedness that is not fretted by foolish fears nor weakened by wistful thinking. It means clear-headedness which sees the causes of war and the values worth defending. It means stout-heartedness which fortifies men with faith and sustains them with endurance. The maintenance of morale requires lofty ideals which serve as guiding stars in the dark nights of the soul, and also definite standards which hold men to their daily duties. It requires well-articulated and smoothly running social organizations which enable men to do together what none can do by himself. The strong-

[1] Westbrook Pegler, *New York World-Telegram*, January 18, 1943.

est nations tomorrow will not be those with the largest stand
ing armies, but those with the most upstanding citizens—
mentally alert, morally responsible, spiritually sensitive, socially
co-operative.

We must remember that the ramparts we watch must be
defensible both from within and without. In every country
and at all times there are those eager to lead the masses in
ways of violence. These potential fomenters of strife can be
rendered innocuous only by preventing the many from feeling
that they are subject to power which is exercised without regard to their welfare and which condemns them to inequities
and indignities. To insure domestic tranquillity is a major way
to provide for the common defense. Trouble at home often
makes for a pernicious foreign policy. When a government
feels itself shaking, a favorite expedient is to conjure up an
outside peril in order to provide a scapegoat or to unite the
warring factions within by means of a common fear.

But in watching our ramparts we must keep our eyes on
the morale of the nations around us. In our fluid world we
can no more isolate ourselves from the currents which surge
through other countries than we can fence an oyster bed
against the waves and the tides of the sea. When communism
takes over Russia, fellow travelers appear on the sidewalks
of New York. When Mussolini injects his dynamic fascism
into the anemic body of Italy, many admirers advocate the
fascist principles for America's disorders. Ours is a day of
warring ideas and ideologies. We wrestle primarily "not
against flesh and blood, but against principalities, against powers, against the rulers of the darkness of this world, against
spiritual wickedness in high places." Against the assault of
ideas the only adequate defense is "the whole armor of God,"
with its girdle of truth, its breastplate of righteousness to pro-

tect the heart, and its helmet of salvation to safeguard the mind. We cannot ward off the germs of error with bayonets or destroy disruptive doctrines with bombers.

If we are to preserve the democratic way of life in those countries now enjoying it, we shall do so only by making democracy so dynamic and efficient that subversive ideas will not flourish therein. We cannot fence a garden against the seeds which blow into it from the weed patch adjoining; we can keep the weeds out by cultivating the garden. And we should remember that America is now surrounded by nations, some of which are going to seed and others of which are younger and more dynamic than our democracy. Russia's youthful zeal, now heightened by military successes, makes her a contagious companion whose germs of culture may find headquarters in the lands left plowed by the retreating heel of Hitler. And if the United States is to co-operate with Russia as she must, she can do so with safety to herself only as she develops a comparable zeal and creativity. Satisfactory co-operation is impossible between two nations when one is dynamic and the other is static.

Is there not still another way of defending our democratic way of life? Can we not keep the weeds out of our yards by cleaning the jungle patches around them? It was on this principle that we tried to proceed after the first World War. We would make the world safe for democracy by stamping the democratic pattern on surrounding countries. Elihu Root headed a commission to Russia which ended its visit with the conclusion that the Russians should adopt a constitution and form of government modeled after ours. Germany, whose people were untrained to habits of free public discussion and civic initiative, was virtually elbowed into forming a republic on the pattern of western democracies.

Similar misguided attempts may be made again. Many who mouth the palatable expression "the American century" entertain the pleasing prospect of a world taking its orders and its order from America. It is an idle dream. Our broken world cannot be united on an American pattern, or by Anglo-Saxon policy. Domination by democracy is in itself a contradiction. The genius of democracy is in its willingness to welcome the emergence of new capacities and new varieties. In the democratic way of life men learn to live with differences. They are hospitable to the potentialities resident in others. If we Americans wish to show ourselves a true democracy, we shall not try to make over the Oriental or the Russian into our mold, but we shall welcome all cultural manifestations which go along with a respect for human dignity. The dignity of man is democracy's standard of measurement. Wherever this dignity is destroyed by servitude, poverty, or other causes, we of the democracies should seek to restore it. Toward that end we should share our goods, our experience, our gospel. But the method of aid should be one of sharing and not of control. And our aim should be to help other peoples to develop themselves in their way, not in ours.

FOUNDATIONS FOR THE PILLARS OF PEACE

The "Six Pillars of Peace" as formulated by the commission instituted under the Federal Council of the Churches of Christ in America are so significant that, like the Deuteronomic commandments, they deserve to be written on our doorposts and our gates. Paralleled now by the new Declaration of Principles published by leaders of the Roman Catholic, Jewish, and Protestant faiths, they show the common denominator of religious demands regarding the postwar settlement. These, added to recent Congressional action, give confident hope that America has turned her back upon the selfish and irresponsible isolationism of the past.

Political collaboration between nations, economic and financial collaboration, adaptation of the world's treaty structures to changing conditions, assurance of ultimate autonomy for subject peoples, control of armaments, establishment of the principle of the rights of people everywhere to intellectual and religious liberty—these are essential pillars of the new peace structure. But what of the foundations to support these pillars?

We are more clearly awake to the need for brotherhood than ever before. Our machine culture has made our world into a neighborhood, and nearness without brotherhood breeds dangers. We of the white race realize that we are outnumbered by the colored races of the world, and after Bataan and Singapore and Burma we fear that unless we come to some better understanding with those increasingly self-conscious races we whites may be a suppressed minority.

But we still treat this matter of brotherhood as a problem to be solved rather than a feeling to be experienced. We flock to the Foreign Policy Association luncheons, but the Russians remain problems to be discussed rather than brothers to be loved. The task before us is to translate our awareness of the need of co-operation into a feeling of fellowship.

We must advance from world outlooks to world insight and sympathy. Our boys will come back from Sicily and the South Seas, from Africa and the Orient, to the farms and villages of America. Their sights will have been lifted. Their contacts will have broadened their knowledge. Competent observers tell us that the men of the fighting forces are putting great hopes for peace in the better opportunities for international travel and acquaintanceship after the war. "They maintain that war can be made impossible if all the peoples of the world really see each how the other lives and works and that now at last, thanks to the airplane, that will be perfectly feasible in a very few years' time." [2] Undoubtedly such physical contact will help toward mutual understanding. But we must remember the tourist's tendency to snap judgments and lazy generalizations. And we cannot forget how many soldiers came back from the last war with fixed prejudices against their former allies. Mere travel and touch of shoulder do not guarantee understanding mind and warm heart.

Desirable indeed is the multiplication of contacts among peoples. But if superficial knowledge is to become sympathetic understanding, we must go deeper. Some time after the first World War political leaders in southeastern Europe conceived a plan to bring the distraught Balkan peoples into closer unity. A great festival was held in Athens. The marble stadium was the scene of sports and speechmaking. One spectator, Professor George Michaelides, tells how thrilled he was at the sight and how he expressed his delight to a member of the Greek parliament who had helped to promote the festival. With a sad smile the member replied: "Do you think this is great? I don't! We politicians are responsible for it, but in planning it we left out God. What we do cannot last. There is too much selfishness and opportunism in the air. We need firmer foundations." [3] That scene in Athens reminds us of the inadequacy of secular methods for fostering world friendship. We did promote international sports. In 1936 we held the last Olympic games in Berlin, and we had planned the next ones for Tokyo. But it takes something deeper than the good fellowship of sports to hold the world together.

[2] Hilary A. St. George Saunders, *New York Times,* August 22, 1943.
[3] *Christian Century Pulpit,* January, 1941, p. 7.

We were also making headway toward brotherhood along the lines of international business. The International Chamber of Commerce was gaining in influence. Its committees were functioning in all leading countries. Its last meeting at Copenhagen saw vast possibilities of co-operation opening up, but also saw the avalanche of war, which it was powerless to stop. Business leaders are giving far more intelligent study than twenty-five years ago to their part in postwar reconstruction and peace planning. And nonpolitical business leadership, organized within nations, will probably be more potent than political agencies in preserving the peace. But it is idle to suppose that enlightened self-interest, with an eye to preserving prosperity, can forestall future wars. Mars releases blind furies which cause self-interest to lose its enlightenment.

And profoundly as I believe that the United States should have joined the League of Nations, I am not sure that even our membership could have saved it from deterioration in the moral weather of the last twenty-five years. It tried to function in an atmosphere of mutual distrust. The League of Nations never had a fair chance. And let us beware lest its failure destroy our faith in some form of world organization. Isolationists will use Geneva as a warning against future co-operation, and conservatives will fall back into their old habit of cautioning against attempts at utopia until we have "changed the hearts of men." Let us realize that the effort to set up such instruments helps to change men's hearts. Concrete reforms cannot wait until men are good enough to work them. The reformation of men is aided by their efforts to work reforms, even though they fail. Some league or federation principle is imperative; and we must make a start, even if it be with imperfect instruments. The alternative is so terrible that nations must co-operate even to the yielding of sovereignty at certain points. But let us give our next effort at world government a fair chance of success by providing what the Greek parliament member called "firmer foundations."

And now we ask what "firmer foundation" would have been given to these efforts at world brotherhood if, as the Greek said, we had not "left out God." For one thing, divine fatherhood becomes the foundation for human brotherhood. When Jesus was asked what is the great commandment in the law, he answered, "Thou shalt love the Lord thy God with all thy heart, and with all thy soul, and with all thy mind." And then he added, "The second is like unto it. Thou shalt love thy neighbor as thyself." It is no accident that they stand together. We cannot sincerely say that we love God unless we love our brother. And we cannot keep loving our brother unless we first say "Father."

When the dignity of the individual derives from the fatherhood of God, it gives a universality which lifts it above parochial likes and dislikes, above color lines and national boundaries. One phenomenon of the current war is the greater antipathy felt by the general public toward the Japanese than toward the Germans or the Italians, while the latter were fighting us. If this be explained by the dastardly attack on Pearl Harbor before war was declared, the explanation is still unsatisfactory. Pearl Harbor did not differ in principle from the German invasion of Poland or Mussolini's stab in the back of France. Is our bitterness toward Japan due to the fact that she struck us and we feel our injuries more than those of Poland or France or England? Or is the hatred of the "Japs" due to their difference in color which lends credence to reports of cruelty and barbarism? No doubt there is something of both factors in our feeling, and both reveal the parochialism and prejudice to which we are prone. We tend to dislike the unlike, to suspect the strange. From this, Christlike love delivers us. In Christ there is no East or West, no bond or free, no white or yellow. In his view we are all equal before God.

The divine evaluation of the individual soul must get into the atmosphere of culture if racial barriers are to be removed. The feeling of superiority is ingrained in the white race; social polish smoothes the surface, but the grain shows beneath. When the Japanese proved such good marksmen at Pearl Harbor, we Americans jumped to the conclusion that the invaders must have been led by German officers. We could not credit the little yellow men with a skill equal to that of the whites. And the sufferings of the Chinese have not aroused us as did the bombings of Britain.

While Madame Chiang's visit to America went far to win new respect for her gallant countrymen, generally speaking, we are still a long way from a feeling of equality with the Chinese. The alert Chinese know it, and the peace table may show it. China's First Lady received an ovation from our Congress surpassing that ever accorded to any other person, any president or foreign ruler; and yet as she left that cheering body, every legislator present knew that if Madame Chiang applied for citizenship in our republic, she could not be admitted. The proposal to repeal the Chinese Exclusion Act has now been made, and no doubt will be passed. That will be a major advance. But Dr. Roy L. Smith sobered a recent audience by reminding it that Russia after this war would have a billion and a quarter orientals behind her, because in the Soviet domain there are representatives of every racial group, all living together without racial discrimination. The Orientals, he said, know that; and they also know about our Harlems and our Detroits.

Sympathetic understanding between races and nations is so much more subtle than the factors affected by laws and leagues. It is a matter of mutual respect, of subconscious attitudes. A group of Negro and white pastors was in recent conference over the Harlem situation. The Negro leaders made it clear that the unrest there would not be cured by improving recreational facilities or even housing conditions. One distinguished colored minister said, "I will give you an illustration of what irritates us." Then he proceeded to recount this experience, in substance: "My wife and I were on a trip from New York to Montreal this summer. We sat on the west side of the train going up the Hudson in order to view the scenery. Then after we passed Troy, we changed to the other side of the car to enjoy the Berkshires on the east. As we moved across the car, a white woman got up and removed her fur piece from the rack above our heads." He added, "Such a gesture of distrust would never have been made had we been white."

Helpfulness cannot effectively flow from the white race to the colored races as a stream flows from a higher source to a lower, but rather it must move as the tide moves across the bosom of the deep, on the level, drawn by the attraction of a power above. That power above which can move love on the level is the power of God as revealed in the spirit of Christ. This transforming, lifting power comes through the creation of a new mental atmosphere. And this involves the steady impact of thought, the repeated sensitizing of the imagination. Here is the point at which the church plays such a crucial part. The church gathers its members in their parish places of worship week after week to pray unto God the Father of all mankind. If the worship is sincere, those sanctuaries are like rooms with mirrors in the ceilings. The worshiper looks up into the mirror above and thereby is enabled the better to see down into the places of those around him. By praying to the Father of all, the devout worshiper in Kokomo or Miami gets a more sympathetic understanding of how life looks to the man along the Burma Road or in Tokyo or Calcutta, in Moscow or London or Berlin. And this practice repeated often enough does give a world outlook and, what is more, a world sympathy.

And the power of the church comes not only through the regularity of its sensitizings, but through its myriad points of application. A few million soldiers will gain new world outlooks by service on foreign fields. Cheap travel after the war may make possible a widening of personal contacts among the nations, but the contacts will still be among the fortunate few. Trade will, no doubt, become world conscious and, let us hope, more co-operative; but the touches of trade often leave sore spots. But over and beyond all these the church is the magic carpet which transports the local villager to the cities of the Orient, which enables a day laborer in Indiana to help a toiler in India, which makes world citizens out of tethered bookkeepers and the untraveled poor.

Among the cultural agencies available for creating a brotherly atmosphere after the war the church is the most promising. Tragic as are its divisions, it is steadily gaining a new sense of world solidarity. With various movements under way pointing toward organic union between several denominations, with the Federal Council of the Churches of Christ progressively cementing the American churches into closer unity, with a World Council of Churches already at work preparing to welcome the co-operation of the Christian bodies in the conquered countries after the war, and with reports of eagerness for a new spirit of brotherhood coming from the churches in the Axis countries—with these signs already manifest, the church gives promise of unprecedented leadership in the work of postwar reconstruction. During the war days it has shown a new statesmanship in studying the conditions of a just and durable peace. It will be a minority force, but it will be the largest, the best organized, and the most farseeing minority group in the peacemaking picture. The church may not officially be given a place at the peace table; but if it lives up to its opportunity and present promise, its influence will be too pervasive for diplomats to ignore.

Furthermore, the church of Christ can condition the atmosphere of the peacemaking by the spirit of forgiveness characteristic of its founder. Credit should be given to the church for helping to keep the spirit of bitterness out of this present war. The sermons of this war breathe a nobler spirit than those of twenty-five years ago. Pulpit prayers seek guidance to be on God's side instead of bumptiously assuming that God is on our side.

In this freedom from hatred the fighting forces have set a good example for those at home. John Steinbeck voices the mood of the young fighters now ordered to turn their technical skill to the business of killing: "This . . . is a war of finding the target in the cross hairs of the bombsight and setting the release, and it isn't a war of speeches and frothy hatred. It is a technical job, a surgeon's job. There is only time for hatred among civilians." [4] The high techniques of war have lengthened the distance between fighters. Combats between bombers do not breed the emotions aroused by hand-to-hand bayonet struggles. But the mitigation of personal hatred is due to something more than the improvement of the killing

[4] John Steinbeck, *Bombs Away: The Story of a Bomber Team*, Viking Press, 1942, p. 66.

technique. It is due to a deeper understanding and a clearer, cooler reflection. The fighters know that the men they fight have nothing personal against them.

And the civilians back home, while they "have time for hatred," have not yet indulged in it with the ferocity of the last war; for the peace education of the past twenty years has opened the eyes of some blind prejudices. As the casualties increase, the bitterness may mount. But we believe the church has shown a new understanding and will lead in creating a spirit of forgiveness which will keep the next peace treaty from being vitiated by the motives of vengeance. At last we are seeing something of the spirit of Him who on the cross, as the nails pierced his palms, could say, "Father, forgive them; for they know not what they do."

THE CONVERSION OF POWER

Already as our victorious forces advance, our military might is being converted into merciful service. In North Africa, Sicily, Italy, and elsewhere our soldiers are being transformed into police and our tanks are giving way to canteens. This work of policing, relief, and reconstruction will have to be continued for an indefinite period. It is a delicate task, and its success will depend even more on the spirit in which it is done than on the material resources made available for the impoverished peoples. We can so conduct ourselves as conquerors that we shall be regarded as saviors from the devastation of the dictators; or we can so turn the population against us that they will think of us, rather than of Hitler and Mussolini, as their oppressors.

An adequate police force will have to be maintained in the postwar world. Whatever international political machinery is set up, it must have power to enforce its sanctions. Until such organization is effected, the United Nations will have to create a pool of power to control the unruly elements of the disordered world. We need humility and divine help if such force is to be exercised with any semblance of justice. And even if we should achieve an unprecedented degree of impartiality and justice, we cannot build a worthy order on the basis of police power. We face the test of converting power *over* into power *for*.

"Ye know that the princes of the Gentiles exercise dominion over them, and they that are great exercise authority upon them. But it shall not be so among you: but whosoever will be great among you, let him be your minister." Mastery by domination is quick, but it is also short-lived, for the subjects are made restless and eager to throw off the yoke. Rome enslaved her conquered peoples and then feared her slaves. Hitler bids fair to repeat Rome's blunder.

On the other hand there is a mastery through service which binds together the server and the served. The Christian church went into China a century ago to share the benefits of Christian culture. Japan's invasion of China has been more rapid; but long after Tojo's hordes are driven out the ambassadors of Christ will remain, respected and welcomed by the people they have served. "The Son of man came not to be ministered unto, but to minister." For that reason Christ has survived the Caesars who ruled at his birth and will outlast the dictators of our day.

And in so far as we of the victor nations and the white race exercise power in the spirit of the ministering Christ, we provide for the common defense of ourselves and the whole family of God.

promote the general Welfare

A government might insure domestic tranquillity and provide for the common defense and yet not help its people to progress. Tranquillity and security may be static—although not for long in our changing world. The welfare of a people demands a dynamic element. The government must not only provide for growth but promote it. The framers of our Federal Constitution could not foresee the future, but they planned that this new nation should have its frontiers flexible toward the tomorrows.

Their tomorrows, now our yesterdays, have seen government assuming ever-widening powers in the promotion of general welfare. From such obviously necessary measures as the establishment of a postal system and the provision for uniform coinage and currency the government has gone on to flood control and then on to relief of unemployment and old-age pensions. And now whither tomorrow? As living grows more complex, we can expect more social compulsions designed to promote the general welfare. As to concrete programs, we have neither the temerity to predict nor the space and ability to discuss. Our purpose here, as elsewhere in this book, is to point out issues and principles which are crucial in the creation of atmosphere for the desired objectives.

WHERE INDIVIDUAL ENTERPRISE MEETS GROUP ACTION

A focal point to be watched in the promotion of the general welfare is the proper relation of individual effort to group action. The question is, How can the individual be sufficiently socialized without being victimized by the group? Public welfare cannot be left to the hit-and-miss methods of private helpfulness prompted by personal impulse. Organization is an accepted principle in industry, in labor, in philanthropy, in relief. But the trend is to create a meshwork of organizations through which individual initiative and responsibility slip out. Government relief, necessary as it often is, cannot be an adequate substitute for private charity. Nor can corporate private philanthropy completely replace the personal delivery of the milk of human kindness. Giving under compulsion does not create charitableness. And receiving help in the spirit of collecting a debt demoralizes the recipient.

In any activity the element of personal creative participation is essential to the enjoyment and value of it. I recall that my own interest in chemistry was very tepid until I was sent into the laboratory to perform some experiments. There I blew up some test tubes and sometimes burned my fingers, but I came to like the study of chemistry. In the church this same principle is to be seen. One reason that young people lose interest in the church is that we fail to combine laboratory practice with the lecture method. We teach them precepts and facts in Sunday school. We preach to them in crowds. But we so seldom have the genius to furnish them with laboratories in which they can work out religious principles in relation to vital issues. Zestful endeavor in every realm requires an opportunity for personal participation, for the exploratory spirit, for the pioneering urge.

How is this personal zest to be preserved in the midst of growing organization? We cannot go back to what some have in mind when they call for "rugged individualism," for they desire an individualism satisfactory only to the rugged. Our nation, if she is our "mother country" as we call her, must be concerned for the weak as well as the strong. Since we are not all equal, as the rugged individualist vociferously claims when he clamors for his rights, the nation, like the mother, must not hold the five-talent citizen back to the pace of his one-talent brother; but she must see that the road is kept open for them both in their pursuit of happiness. Since we cannot go back to unorganized individualism, we must seek to promote individual initiative and enterprise by going beyond group organization. Private enterprise must be enterprising enough to do things better than governments can do them if it wishes to stave off regimentation. Unless, for example, business and industry have the wisdom and the willingness to provide jobs for our returning soldiers, the demobilized millions will demand that the government try its hand at the task. Since Christian civilization and our own America in particular are committed "to promote the general welfare," the only way forward is for individual citizens and private enterprise to be more Christian and more enterprising than the government.

Group organization is not necessarily stifling to individual initiative. The fact that you are only one citizen in a nation of 132,000,000 need not paralyze your sense of responsibility for your government nor your sense of participation in it. The size of America should thrill you; the magnitude of her public activities multiplies your possible points of service, and her organizations not only preserve that law and order which give you freedom but also the openings which give you participation. The fact that you work in a factory with five thousand employees and belong to a labor union need not destroy your initiative. To be sure, there is a tendency to be dwarfed by the presence of numbers; but if you have sufficient self-respect and social spirit, the very numbers increase your horizons of outlook and your contacts for influence. The fact that you belong to a church of two thousand members does not necessarily regiment you into a conventional religion. Just as the health of the whole body aids in the healing of an injured organ, so the sense of belonging to the body of Christ sends a surge of strength into your wavering spirit, and the organizations of the church put longer levers of service into your hands.

However congested the roads may be with organizations, the individual, if he is enterprising and Christian enough, can find a way to go "the second mile" beyond group action. And such individuals, both in great spheres and in small, are the advance guard in promoting the general welfare.

WHERE THE SPIRIT OF SCIENCE MEETS THE SPIRIT OF SERVICE

At the mention of general welfare our minds turn at once to the contribution of science. We think of science as the handmaid of progress. We are ever being reminded how many mechanical slaves science has put at the service of each modern person. We recall the drudgery from which man's inventive genius has delivered us. We of the advanced countries pride ourselves on our high standards of living, which we ascribe to our scientific methods of production.

Our Western culture has been proceeding on the principle of pursuing happiness through the production of comforts and conveniences. We have multiplied machine power, shortened hours of work, developed painless surgery, improved our housing. Yet comfort has not brought harmony. As a writer with a cynical but sharp eye has pointed out, the divorce rate has risen in about the same ratio as the increase in the sale of vacuum cleaners. And the twentieth century, which we boastfully called "the century of progress" at a great exposition ten years ago, has shown the worst war record in all history.

Scientific progress has paradoxically increased our sense of power and also our feeling of helplessness. As we travel across the country, we are thrilled at the sight of throbbing factories and the seemingly endless production lines of war material; and then our train stops, and a company of draftees come aboard, leaving on the platforms parents who look so helpless. We are caught in systems which seem to clip our powers. Have we created a Frankenstein machine culture which we are no longer able to control?

To be sure, the spirit of science gives hope of promoting the general welfare. The scientist calmly pursuing his search for truth amid the blusterings of political forces and the blitzkriegs of war seems a beacon of hope in a dark world. The universality of scientific formulas and principles suggests that unity of interests which can bind common humanity across the present chasms of our broken society. When Harvard celebrated her tercentenary with an unprecedented conclave of scientists, one observer was thrilled by the thought of the actual and potential brotherhood which the search for truth fosters. There sat the leaders of thought drawn from lands which only recently had been embattled and were even then girding for another war. But nationality was no barrier to the free exchange of thought. There was to be seen an imperialism of truth transcending the imperialism of nations. Could not this spirit be spread until on a vast cultural scale the Master Teacher's prediction might be realized: "Ye shall know the truth, and the truth shall make you free"—free from the provincialisms, the prejudices, the suspicions, the hatreds, which devastate the world?

I recall attending one of the mathematics sessions. A lecturer was demonstrating an intricate proposition in the theory of numbers. As he brought his involved demonstration to a successful conclusion, he remarked that if anyone should ask the value of his solution, it should be answered that its chief value was that it had no value. (I recall that remark because it was the only one which I could understand in the entire discussion.) Here was revealed the motivation of pure science—the search after truth for its own sake. The purity of such a motive in our ultilitarian, money-minded world is as refreshing as the sight of Popocatepetl's snowy summit from the dusty roads of Mexico.

But the purity of pure science has proved too weak to resist the seductions of our competitive and utilitarian world. Most of the scientists who sat together at Harvard's tercentenary in 1936 have since been serving their respective countries in producing the means of mutual destruction. This subservience of science shows that "pure intellect alone is no effective tool in preserving righteousness in the world, and this fact, it must be said to his discredit, was before the war perhaps generally unrecognized by the average brilliant scientist." [1]

The scientist may pride himself that his function is to find the formula or perfect the process and that any concern for the use to which his findings are put is a reflection on the purity of science. But such pride has proved itself the kind which goeth before a fall. The scientist must concern himself with values and uses. "He must gain a feeling for the pulse of human society, must be able to think in terms of the hearts as well as of the heads of common man, must acquire the

[1] Caryl P. Haskins in *Science, Philosophy and Religion*, Second Symposium, Conference on Science, Philosophy and Religion in Their Relation to the Democratic Way of Life, Inc., 1942, p. 4.

intimate understanding of the ways of the human social organism and the vision in human affairs of the great statesman. Most important of all, he must exercise this knowledge in the actual capacity and practice of great human leadership, and at the same time must preserve his present training and ideals and outlook intact in the research and technical fields which now are his own. For, if he is to be successful, it is vital that he be at once a great scientist and a great humanist." [2]

How many scientists will hear and heed such a call to service it is too early to predict. Significant is it that leaders in the scientific field have been joining with leaders of philosophy and religion in conference to study their relation to the democratic way of life. If and when science assumes its responsibility for values, then the resultant enhancement of values will react to spur science. The marriage of the spirit of science and the spirit of service breeds both a renaissance and a reformation. Listen to a distinguished anthropologist: "The Chinese discovered vaccination centuries ago, but had no use for the saving of life in a culture where life as such was not yet valued. It took Christian emphasis upon the value of the individual human life coinciding with discovery of vaccination before that discovery could be turned to service of men." [3] When science becomes inspired with a Christlike sense of human values, who can set a limit to its service in promoting the general welfare?

WHERE EXPERTS ERR

Promising as would be the marriage of the spirit of science and the spirit of service, some guidance would be required in the rearing of their children.

[2] *Ibid.,* pp. 10-11.
[3] Margaret Mead, *And Keep Your Powder Dry,* W. Morrow & Co., 1942. p. 231.

In his concern for human values, the scientist is handicapped by his specialization. Our fields of scientific knowledge call for such intensive cultivation that their expert workers often fail to look over the fences of their own specialty; and when they do, they so often make fools of themselves. The specialist is prone to lack that quality which Matthew Arnold attributed to Sophocles—that he saw life steadily and saw it whole. It should be remembered that a view of the whole helps in understanding the parts. Specialization without largeness of outlook is self-defeating.

Furthermore, there are some areas of experience in which professionalism avails not, but rather does it become a hindrance. Mr. Chesterton maintains, and with some point, that specialists are always wrong when they leave their own particular fields and impose their methods on what he would call "the rich and reeking human personality." If we want a library catalogued or an office system overhauled, we call in experts. But when a person is on trial for his life, we leave his fate in the hands of a jury of his peers—not a group of penologists or policemen or lawyers who live constantly in the courtroom atmosphere, but men and women brought in from the ordinary walks of life. Our jury system is based on the belief that persons with a fresh, unprofessional wholeness of outlook are the best judges of the motives, the innocence and the guilt, of their fellow men.

The errors of experts call for correction if the general welfare is to be promoted. The supposedly wise become blind in their own conceits. Looking for the earmarks of learning, they reject simple truth which bears not the stamp of approved institutions. Narrowed by tradition, scholars are prone to scorn new channels of knowledge. There is an academic snobbery which views the man on the street as a moron and belittles the teacher who tries to popularize his subject. The Galileos, the Pasteurs, the Curies were not welcomed by their fellow scientists but rather had to run the gantlet of their ridicule. In the stoning of the prophets, an all-too-conspicuous part has been played by those who themselves were looked up to for their learning. A scholar who had taken part in the stoning of new teachers later came to confess that "God hath chosen the foolish things of the world to confound the wise." And it was the expert's tendency to error which made the Master Teacher say, "I thank thee, O Father, Lord of heaven and earth, because thou hast hid these things from the wise and prudent, and hast revealed them unto babes."

Then, too, our modern experts tend to err in their estimate of power as well as of truth. Our dynamic industrial civilization dazzles us with its development of mechanical power. From the millrace where our grandfathers ground their flour to Boulder Dam, which furnishes power and light for millions; from the village blacksmith's shop under the spreading chestnut tree to the Ford factory under the acres of roof at Willow Run; from the sailing ships in which admirals now living took their training to the giant airplane carriers now under their command—all these are developments of power which make Aladdin's lamp look like a cigar lighter.

But in our perfection of mechanical power we tend to fall under its spell. We tend to be impressed by big, noisy, speedy forces. This is the era of "the strong man," the bluster of bigness, the mania of speed. But we fail to see the limitations of this kind of power. "Not by might, nor by power, but by my spirit, saith the Lord of hosts" is a truth which our time forgets. The plane with its speed of two hundred miles per hour lacks the power to heal the breaking heart of the passenger it carries. Fleets of bombers may give control of the air over a country, but they cannot purge a land of its trade barriers and race prejudices. The heightening of our industrial horsepower does not improve the inner initiating factors of manpower. And when giant power is given to men with pygmy motives, the result is likely to be a runaway resulting in disorganized production, dislocated markets, disaffected workers, and devastating wars.

A few years ago a schoolboy of twelve, my own son, wrote some lines which he called "Contemplation of the Sea After the Battle of Jutland." After describing the mighty warships in their battling fury, he closed:

> For a few brief hours they held sway,
> And now destroyed by themselves
> They lie in thine unfathomable depths,
> Whilst thou rollest tranquilly on.
> Are they not like man striving for power throughout the ages
> And at last being engulfed by the relentless elements?

The lad's insight was true. Man struts his time upon earth's stage, boasts his strength, brandishes his arms, builds his battleships; then, when his bluster is over, nature's quiet forces have the last word. It is these quiet forces which the modern experts in power fail to appraise. It is the silent strength which fools the specialist. The silent pressure of personal influence; the lifting power of a little child's presence in a home; the cleansing force of innocent gladness, as when a "Pippa" passes; the world-shaking strength of a frail hunchback like William Wilberforce when he is charged with a great purpose; the life-changing shadow of the cross—such are the forces which our technically trained, machine-minded

experts fail to measure. And if science is to show its possibilities in the promotion of the general welfare, it must correct
the errors of its experts by a cultivation of these spiritual forces
which it has scorned.

The wiser among our scholars and scientists are increasingly
aware of this needed widening of outlook. "Means must be
found to interpret scholars not only to one another but
also to men of affairs outside the field of scholarship;
and, on the other hand, to interpret to the scholar
more clearly than has ever been done the problems of the
man of affairs." [4] Silly and stupid is the present breach between "men of affairs" and what they sarcastically call "the
brain trust." To be sure, the role of college professors in guiding public affairs has not been marked by brilliance. But
neither has been the service of those hardheaded realists of
the market place whose operating theory is that "business is
business" and is to be run by ethical standards peculiar to its
province. If the academic circles need contact with the reali-
ties of the street, it is equally true that the realists of business
need contact with the ideals and ethics which should reside in
the universities.

What is it to be a "man of affairs"? The question recalls a
dining-car conversation with an energetic and bristling business executive during the depression days of the early 1930's.
He declared that the trouble with America was that it had too
much "overhead" and too few producers. This assertion
aroused sympathetic interest, for it raised visions of our ex-
cessive governmental overhead and bureaucratic burdens. But
then he went on in this tenor: "Think of the nonproductive
overhead we are carrying. Think of the artists, the musicians,

[4] Statement of the Conference on Science, Philosophy and Religion, *New York Times*, September 1, 1942.

the writers, the teachers, the lawyers, the preachers"—and he proceeded to list about all the workers with nonmaterial things as nonproductive. Where is a civilization tending when it thinks the creators of material things are the only ones who merit the title of producers?

Near the railroad station at Chester, Pennsylvania, is an electric sign blazing forth these words: "What Chester Makes, Makes Chester." That is a good sign, provided its meaning is sufficiently inclusive. If, as we fear, it means the articles manufactured in the industrial city of Chester, it is not true. But if it means the boys and girls, the homes and characters, then it is true that "what Chester makes, makes Chester." Human values are a city's main product, and the making of them is a community's basic industry. But what city pays its schoolteachers as well as its engineers?

Yes, the scientists and the scholars need to cultivate collaboration with the "men of affairs." But let us remember that the workers with ideas and ideals, the forgers of the flaming words of prophecy, the makers of homes and trainers of children, the creators of good will in fraternal and community circles, the custodians of the spiritual crises of life and death —these too are "men of affairs." The task before us is not merely the mending of broken national boundaries, the restoration of markets, the reconstruction of bombed cities, the setting up of a new international order. The task which confronts our day of destiny is the unifying of a shattered culture, the creation of a society in which the whole man can live a full life.

WHERE TRUSTEES BECOME OWNERS

The sense of trusteeship necessary for promoting the general welfare must extend beyond the leaders of science, philosophy, and religion to the citizenry at large. A man of honor exercises more care in handling trust funds than in managing his own property. Our laws are geared to the same principle. We have strict regulations as to what investments are legal for trust funds. But this sense of honor expected in the handling of private trusts by no means applies to the popular attitude toward public trusts. Hence the waste and extravagance which so often attend government ownership and operation. Hence the easier conscience with which citizens will cheat an impersonal government than a personal acquaintance. Hence the contrast between the energetic forethought given by the individual to his own affairs and his laxity toward the interests of things held in common.

Stanley Jones tells of walking through one of the old sections of an Oriental city. To a friend with him he remarked about the contrast between the electrically lighted and beautifully clean shops and the narrow, dirty streets which ran in front of them. The gentleman explained: "Don't you understand? These shops belong to the men inside, but these streets do not belong to anybody, so all throw their filth from the shops into the streets." Such is the selfish propensity of human nature. What is everybody's business is nobody's business.

A heightened and tightened sense of public trusteeship is necessary if we are to look after the streets as well as the shops, if we are to give the same care to public business as to private business.

Mere moral exhortation, however, will not achieve this heightened sense of trusteeship. We must lead men back to the basic Christian conception of the nature of property. From the Christian point of view property is never static but always functional. "Economic resources are the God-given means and media of fellowship. They are not first of all private possessions, but rather responsibilities entrusted to man by God for the sake of the common welfare. Property belongs, first of all, to God, has been given by Him for social purposes, and no individual or group is ever more than a steward of it." [5] A religious sense of stewardship is needed to sharpen the social sense of trusteeship. Men feel more sting when they see a social evil as also a sin against God.

Moreover, there is a transforming light to be shed on this principle of trusteeship. Practical common sense would prompt us to say that a person qualifies for promoting the general welfare by first looking after his own personal welfare. Mind your own business first. The man who is a good manager of his own property is the one who is made a trustee of others' property. The man who makes a success of his private business is put up to hold offices of public trust.

While this principle seems logical, there is a corollary which the Master of Life laid down when he said, "If ye have not been faithful in that which is another man's, who shall give you that which is your own?" That is, we get what belongs to us by serving as trustees of others. Strange as this may seem, there are some areas of life in which this truth becomes apparent. Take it in the home. Suppose a person enters the marital relationship thinking primarily of what he is going to get out of it. In A. S. M. Hutchinson's *This Freedom*, the wife comes to the conclusion that a husband's primary interest in a home is the satisfaction of his possessive instinct. She says: "That's what he marries for—a home, . . . a place where he can have his wife and his children and his

[5] Nels F. S. Ferré, *Return to Christianity*, Harper & Bros., 1943, p. 65.

dogs and his books and his servants and his treasures and his slippers and his ease, and can feel comfortably that she and they and it are his." [6] A home begun on the basis of such possessiveness never yields the dividends it was meant to produce. But when a person marries because he wants to be the trustee of a life more precious than his own, when he says, as did George Herbert Palmer of his wife, "I never called her mine," then he receives a love so rich that it beggars appraisal.

And there are fields other than the family in which the values of possession come to us through first being trustees. Two college contemporaries of mine became members of the same fraternity. One made good use of his fraternity connections for his own advancement. Through fraternity aid he was elected to several campus offices. The other man did not seek the limelight. But whenever there was a brother in difficulty or a thankless committee task to be performed, he was on hand. Today, when the alumni reconvene, it is the latter and not the former around whom they gather. By his fidelity to the interests of others he came at last to possess their affections.

And in the larger sphere of civic life, the basic difference of motives between a politician and a statesman is that the former uses public office for personal advantage while the latter treats his office as a trusteeship of the public good. The politician may get the votes in a particular election, but the statesman holds the hearts and memories.

Can the general citizenry be led to see this principle that the values of personal welfare come through being trustees of the public welfare? Of course, it is high doctrine. And here, as elsewhere, we must approach the ideal by way of the intermediate. Trusteeship can be taught to children through

[6] Little Brown & Co., 1922, p. 228,

home responsibilities, school tasks, and church activities. In school a boy learns the joy of belonging—and sometimes the agony of not belonging. The value of college loyalty is that it calls the student out of himself, links him with something larger than himself, and begets the enriching sense of belonging. Various are the ways of introducing youth to the truth that we get what belongs to us by belonging to something bigger than ourselves.

War brings this sense of trusteeship home to farm and factory, to youth and womanhood; yet it is too costly a price to pay for this lesson. But could we not take the teaching of this trusteeship out of the bloody context of war and continue it in peace? *The youth of America could be drafted for public service in peace time.* A year's time given to public welfare projects by every young citizen would serve to neutralize that self-seeking spirit which so often motivates education. This period of public service might be arranged for vacation seasons. There would have to be some adjustment in cases of youth with dependents, and care would be required to prevent a militaristic perversion of the whole programs. But the difficulties in detail and the delay in private advancement would be more than compensated by the widening of sympathies, the discipline in co-operation, and the heightened spirit of public service.

WHERE NATURE'S FIRST LAW MEETS LIFE'S DEEPEST LAW

Sooner or later, if men are to learn the art of living together, they confront life's deepest law. Embedded in the wisdom of the race is the old maxim, "Self-preservation is nature's first law." But through blood and sweat and tears man has learned that the law of self-preservation has to be linked with the principle of co-operation. In the jungle, animals herd together. Savages live in tribes. Civilized men form nations. And modern men are now being forced to accept international associations. Also man has learned that there is something in the heart which at times supersedes the law of self-preservation with the principle of vicarious sacrifice. There is a love which makes a mother starve for her brood and a man lay down his life for his friends. There is an honor of the service which sends firemen into burning buildings to rescue strangers and causes soldiers to stand at their posts in the face of death.

While we recognize the outcropping of this deeper law of vicarious sacrifice in the heroic moments of life, we nevertheless assume that the general level of living is the law of self-preservation—each man for himself and the devil take the hindmost. Our civil laws and civic institutions are geared to the principle that man's ordinary motivation is self-interest. Even the church, if one is to judge from the sermon subjects announced, tries to draw its crowds by appealing to their self-interest, their desire for health, happiness, prosperity, safety. Yet if we are to call ourselves a Christian civilization, we must remember that the central symbol of Christianity is the cross, because the deepest law of our Lord is voluntary redemptive sacrifice. Complex as is contemporary culture, the situation is still in essence what it was when the apostle Paul sent his twofold formula to the Galatian community: "Every man shall bear his own burden," and, "Bear ye one another's burdens, and so fulfill the law of Christ." In the linking of these two laws, not only in heroic moments but in daily living, lies the promotion of the general welfare.

Again it is high doctrine to advocate the principle of vicarious sacrifice as a level of general practice. But pause a minute. Longfellow once likened our nation to a ship:

Thou, too, sail on, O Ship of State!
Sail on, O Union, strong and great!
Humanity with all its fears,
With all the hopes of future years,
Is hanging breathless on thy fate!

Think, if you please, of this nation as a ship. When a ship strikes a mine, what is the principle of action? Is it the Four Freedoms? Is it insistence on the Bill of Rights? Is it each for himself? No, the wounded are placed in the lifeboats first. The officers go last, and the higher the rank the later they go. The honor of the service demands, "Bear ye one another's burdens and so fulfill the law" of the sea, for the law of the sea at that moment runs parallel to the law of Christ. If our nation is a ship of state on which hang "the hopes of future years," then our challenge is to make this law of the sea into the law of the land.

secure the Blessings of Liberty

A free man is more than a freedman. The slave may be manumitted by his master and remain servile still. If it is true that

> Stone walls do not a prison make,
> Nor iron bars a cage,

it is equally true that the removal of such restrictions does not insure liberty.

The inwardness of freedom is not appreciated by our materialistic culture. We seek to free ourselves by getting others out of our way, while we fail to see that we individually may be standing in our own way. We overthrow the bastilles of oppressive governments and then come home to the prisons of our own self-centeredness. We fight to destroy dictators and forget that every form of government seems restrictive to those who have not learned self-control. The spoiled child whines at all family restraint, and the libertine thinks that every rule of moral decency is a narrow, puritanical blue law. No external power can give freedom to the person who has not learned the free use of his own powers. "The price which civilized man pays for freedom is the need for intense effort to organize his life." [1]

In this effort to organize and integrate the self, we have

[1] Statement of Conference on Science, Philosophy and Religion, *loc. cit.*

considered the cohesive power of the Christ spirit. Let us go on to inquire whether he can help the integrated individual to function freely in the group, for we seek not only freedom to follow our own destinies but also freedom for full community.

We have to find our freedom within ever-increasing social pressures. However our spirits may rebel against social restraints, we may as well reconcile ourselves to the fact that we must live in ever closer contact with our fellows. There may be some reallocation of population in order to relieve the pressure in certain countries, and there may be some decentralization of cities through easier travel and better housing. But the physical exits from the crowd are being closed. Measured in time units, the modern world of the twentieth century is smaller than the Mediterranean world of the first century. When no place on the globe is more than sixty hours by air from any other spot, the points of possible isolation are becoming scarcer. When the pioneers of our country lacked elbow room in the East, they went west; but when the migrants of our day move towards the lands of hitherto golden opportunity, they gather "grapes of wrath." Our fathers could stop anywhere on the road and chat with their neighbors, but we are not free to be so friendly on a four-lane motor highway. We must find freedom, if we are to find it, within the crowd.

In considering the contribution of high religion to the blessings of liberty, let us limit ourselves to the "four essential freedoms" which have become so familiar.

FREEDOM OF SPEECH

It requires a Christlike imagination to make freedom of speech appreciated by those of us who have been reared in

America. If we had lived in a society where secret micro-phones were hidden under our desks, where our social circles were honeycombed with spies, where even our sons and daughters might belong to youth organizations which forced them to report the doings of their parents—if such had been our experience, then we would realize the value of free speech. As one refugee from a German-controlled land said, the difference between the life she left and the land to which she had come could be symbolized by doorbells. In the dic-tator-ridden region, the sound of the doorbell made the occupants of the house cringe before the approaching cruelty of the Gestapo. Here it denotes the coming of the friendly postman or the call of a neighbor. But we who have not suffered such things need imaginations sufficiently sensitive to put ourselves in others' places if we are to prize a world where men can say what they think, where the press is free to criticize those in power, where the schools in the search for truth are not perverted by any pressure group. And since it is the Anglo-Saxon influence to which the world must look for the spread of this first freedom, it behooves us who belong to that tradition to value liberty of speech enough to preserve and propagate it.

Furthermore, the role of religion is to make us scan more closely our motives for desiring this freedom of speech. Why do we crave it? Is it just to satisfy the impulsive desire to speak our minds? Or is it because we are sincerely concerned that truth shall prevail? Speech is designed to be a vehicle of thought running between personalities. Language is a two-way traffic between mind and mind. And genuine freedom of speech requires that the road between minds be kept open for the two-lane traffic of thought.

If, therefore, we are genuinely concerned for the interchange of truth, we shall seek to remove the barrier of ignorance which blocks the traffic of free speech. A speaker may be free from any censorship, and yet his speech may deflect the truth. A falsehood told in ignorance may be as fatal in its results as a lie told through propaganda. Rumors spread with good intention may be as dangerous and destructive as those circulated by fifth columnists. Also there is the barrier of prejudice, which like the spider, makes everywhere its home and lives where there seems nothing to live on. Prejudice distorts the truth on the lips of the speaker and deafens the ears of the listener. And, remember, law cannot remove these barriers of ignorance and prejudice. They are too subtle for the censor. They require a spiritual cure. And that is what the Christlike spirit gives. Christ said, "Ye shall know the truth, and the truth shall make you free." His spirit puts an insistence on truth which helps to free men from the ignorance that is content to repeat idle rumors, malicious gossip, distorted half-truths, and unfounded fears. The Christ spirit serves to set men free from the prejudice which closes the mind and inflames the passions.

Unless this insistence on truth is inculcated in both listener and speaker, freedom of speech is not safeguarded. As long as we wish to feel safe and good rather than right and real, and as long as the pulpit, the press, and the radio lack the courage to give people what they need rather than what they want, the vicious circles of falsehood betray our vaunted freedom of speech. The agencies of public opinion may be free from government censorship and yet may be so subservient to popular taste and passion that the results are equally deplorable. These agencies must, of course, keep close enough to the people to catch their interest; but they should ever seek to be sufficiently above the heads of the crowds to keep them looking up. Instead of catering to lust and cheapness, to fears and hatreds, the press, the radio, the screen—yes, also the pulpit—might remember that Lincoln, the man who holds the affections of more common people than probably any other human being, made his appeal to what he called the "better angels of our nature."

Moreover, if freedom of speech is to fulfill its service to truth, there must be a new awareness of the subtle temptations to which it is subjected. The improved means of communication have vastly increased the range and therefore the responsibility of those who use them. The radio speaker has a subtle power of influence never enjoyed by the editor or platform speaker. Listen to this charge made by a contemporary publication: "Radio has in general tried to follow printed journalism's tradition of a free press. But there has been constant trouble. Commentators can and often do convey their own feelings toward news merely by tone of voice. Their daily entrance into 30,000,000 U. S. homes is very intimate and puts a premium on voice rather than on brains or integrity. This accounts for the fact that much of the output of U. S. radio pundits is pontifical tripe." [2] One may not endorse the above conclusions, but he can hardly refute the premise. When free speech is given the facilities of the radio, it must be exercised with a new sensitivity to the subtlety of its influence.

We demand the right of free speech. But does that right warrant our saying publicly anything that comes into our heads? Not at all. If we have the Christlike spirit, even the common sense, to respect the domain of "obedience to the unenforceable," we are restrained by a regard for those who

[2] *Time*, June 28, 1943, p. 42.

hear us. A teacher should consider the capacities and sensibilities of the pupils under his care. A preacher should feel that it is a sin against fair play to say from his privileged pulpit, where men cannot talk back to him, some things which he might feel free to say in private conversation or even in the open forum. If freedom of speech is to be the servant of truth—which it was meant to be—it must be insured by the intelligence, the imagination, the integrity, the social awareness of its advocates. To strengthen these requirements is the role of high religion.

FREEDOM OF WORSHIP

The second of the four "essential freedoms" is also one which we of America fail to appreciate, partly because we take it for granted and partly because we do not take our religious convictions seriously enough. We sing about the "faith of our fathers":

> How sweet would be their children's fate,
> If they, like them, could die for thee!

But one well wonders how many church members would die for their religious faith. Perhaps if some other ethnic religion had sufficient vitality to invade America and Christianity were reduced to a struggling minority, then we might be baptized in the fire and blood of the martyrs. But as it is, our hymns of courage have a hollow sound. We are like marchers in a parade who are too far back to hear the music of the band. While the early Christians at the head of the column marched even to their death with springing step, we shuffle along even to our comfortable churches with sluggish listlessness. We conventional Christians are too far from the sources of the church's heroism to catch the music of the

martyrs. We read about the catacombs of apostolic days and
the bigotry which our colonial settlers left in coming to this
land. But the religious freedom we enjoy cost us nothing,
and until we pay something for it we shall not truly prize it.

But how can we revive the appreciation of religious freedom in a society so refined that physical persecution is hardly
conceivable? Since our culture has become so departmental-
ized and secularized that religion is regarded as just one of
seven or more departments of interest, a person's taste in
religious worship is treated by the public with the same polite
indifference as his taste in music or art. A man runs no more
risk in attending the church of his choice than in preferring
"swing" music to opera. And until religion is vitally linked
with other cultural interests in which men are still intolerant,
religious tolerance will remain an empty and meaningless
term.

But if, for instance, a man's religious affiliations become involved in his political aspirations, religious tolerance may
rise into a real issue. There are cities in which a preponder-
ance of Protestant candidates would kill a party's chances of
winning the election; and there are sections in which a Roman Catholic could not be elected to office. And when religious beliefs are linked to racial relations, then tolerance is
tested, for we are far more tolerant about creeds than about
races. Even in the field of education, religious freedom raises
some real issues. A teacher may worship where she pleases;
but if she does, she may not always teach where she pleases.
And so sharp are the sectarian divisions and suspicions in
some communities that all religious instruction is barred from
the schools lest one sect should secure undue advantage.

Let us then beware of taking our boasted freedom of worship for granted. When our religious connections make con-

tact with interests really vital to us, we are still frighteningly sensitive to the sore spots. We still have a price to pay for real religious freedom.

The test of our courage comes when we are in the minority. The test of our tolerance comes when we are in the majority. In the latter months of 1942 a rather sharp issue arose over the matter of Protestant missions in Latin America. Spokesmen for the Roman Catholic hierarchy in the United States declared that the sending of Protestant missionaries to the lands south of us was a threat to Pan-American friendship and a reflection on the Christian church which had so long dominated those countries. The Federal Council of the Churches of Christ in America countered with the assertion that the Roman Catholic protest was an infringement on religious liberty. Yet Protestants should avoid any pharisaical pride in their open-mindedness, for there are sections of our own land where the building of a Romanist chapel would be bitterly resented. Both situations illustrate the tendencies of religious majorities to become intolerant.

The spirit of Christ must be revived among his followers if religious freedom is to get control of the atmosphere, even of our own America. Religion, to be of vital force, must pervade all areas of cultural interest; and as long as we have economic, racial, political, or other spheres of intolerance, then we still face a costly fight for religious freedom. Christ calls his followers to carry their religious convictions into the issues that really matter to them and give a healing touch to the sore spots of intolerance. He imparts not only the spirit of tolerance which lives and lets live but also the spirit of love which lives and helps live.

No religious body is fit to survive in a free world unless it is willing to submit its creed and contribution to the test of open comparison with the beliefs of other religious bodies. Christ rebuked his disciples when they came to him saying, "We saw one casting out devils in thy name; and we forbade him, because he followed not with us." He replied, "He that is not against us is for us." To Christ it was the spirit and the result that counted, not the label. He was so confident of his cause that he was willing to have his work tested in open sharing. Let us not be afraid to learn the good points of other ethnic faiths. Let there be free exchange of cultural elements between the universities of America and those of China and India. Let both Protestantism and Romanism share their beliefs with Latin America. Christ's test, universal in application, is "Ye shall know them by their fruits." Any sect which fears to face that test should search itself to see whether it is a branch of which Christ is the vine. Christianity has not yet approximated the catholicity that was in Christ. "Other sheep I have, which are not of this fold."

But do we really wish to know and understand other folds? Few Christians have made any study of the other religions, even of Judaism, from which we sprang. Most Protestants get their knowledge of Roman Catholicism only from Protestant sources, and vice versa. We need more light of knowledge to dispel the fog of prejudice, and sufficient imagination to see how life would look to us if we had been born in another religious tradition. The horizon is not without signs of promise. Religious broadcasts are helping to break down the barriers of ignorance and suspicion. The good-will conferences between Roman Catholics, Protestants, and Jews give much promise, especially where they go beyond the mere expressions of respect to the sharing of experiences. The collaboration of chaplains in the present war is begetting a more sympathetic fellowship among the faiths, for mutual regard is heightened more by working together than by talking together.

Out in the West is a road which once led to a silver mine. In earlier days there were bandits in that region, and the road was dangerous. But miners went through. Now the bandits are gone, but the road has fallen into such disrepair that it is virtually impassable. Why? Because the mine has been abandoned. That is a parable of what has happened to religion in some countries, and what could happen in America. In this land of liberty there are no bandits to block the highway of religious worship. Each of us is free to worship in his own way. But if we do not go to worship, and if we do not relate worship to the working activities of daily living, the road of religious freedom will not remain open forever.

Privileges left unused are eventually lost. How did the Russian church lose its freedom? By first losing its vitality and usefulness as a servant of God and the people. And distinguished German refugees have penitently confessed that the church in the Reich was partly responsible for the rise of the Hitler regime because it allowed itself to become divorced from the live problems of the people. When a church ceases to be a house of sincere prayer and a home of good works and becomes an empty shell of form, some outside force is sure to crush it. The primary need in preserving religious liberty is to increase spiritual vitality.

FREEDOM FROM WANT

In the words of President Roosevelt, freedom from want "translated into world terms means economic understandings which will secure to every nation a healthy peacetime life for its inhabitants."

In no country have all people ever had enough to eat, and in some countries famine and death by starvation are ever-present possibilities for vast numbers of human beings. Such conditions are no longer necessary. The means for their control are in men's hands. The bountiful earth can produce food enough for all its inhabitants. When we stop to think that if the globe's entire population were all put in the state of Texas there would be only about twelve to the acre, we realize that the "good earth" is not overcrowded. Then too we have learned the fundamentals of nutrition. We know also how to make two ears of corn grow where one grew before and how to breed fowl that lay not thirty eggs a year but three hundred. And when we consider what the stepped-up production of the war period is revealing of our industrial and agricultural potentialities, our imaginations are made dizzy by the possible technological progress ahead.

Certainly the future offers no legitimate excuse for an economy of scarcity. There are sufficient resources to provide "a healthy peacetime life" for all the sons of men. A few years ago we held before our people a prosperity promising "two cars in every garage and a chicken in every pot." Recent events have inspired cynics to revise this formula so that for the time being it may be said "the chickens are in the garage and the cars have gone to pot." But the present rationing of such material possessions is a war emergency. When the ingenuity of man is redirected from destruction to peacetime production, there will be such a plentitude of products available that the disgrace of undernourished children, unsanitary slums, underprivileged homes, or famines can be removed from the world's landscape—provided the people who have sufficient genius and good will to work out fair means of distributing them. It will be possible to make and grow sufficient things to go around. Can we make them go around?

One hopeful aspect of our day is the intelligent concern now being given to the future food supply. The relief and rehabilitation work already in progress, the United Nations Conference on Food and Agriculture, the lend-lease arrangements, and the various agreements—all these attest a serious intention to tackle the specter of hunger through international co-operation. We are showing determination to open channels which will prevent the repetition of little pigs being slaughtered in one land while little children go hungry in another, of plowing cotton under in America while desperately poor Chinese wrap newspapers around their bare bodies to keep out the cold.

Freedom from want, however, will require more than "economic understandings" between governments. It will call for a spirit of sharing on the part of the people. Britain is proposing to continue its food rationing after the war, partly for the purpose of helping to feed devastated areas; and food experts are working on suggested changes in American eating habits, so that supplies of foods most needed by others may be released to be sent abroad. How will we respond to such proposals of continued rationing after the war? One may well wonder, when he learns that during the past war year, despite all the calls for sacrifice, our civilian per capita food consumption has risen.

Food, however, is not the only essential needed to free men from want. Widespread disease is almost invariably linked with lack of food, and the ravages of preventable disease are now being systematically charted. Trachoma, leprosy, malaria, tuberculosis, smallpox, and cholera flourish where diets are poor and sanitation is lacking. Leprosy alone is estimated to infect three million victims, and only about three per cent of these are receiving any treatment whatever.

The cure for these evils of food shortage and preventable disease is not a permanent dole from an American Santa Claus. The constructive and the Christian approach is to help people everywhere to help themselves in making better use of what they have. This self-help can be developed only through education. Reading is the most basic technique for helping people to understand their place in the world, for teaching them to feed and care for themselves. Steps must be taken to lift the blight of illiteracy which now stunts 97 per cent of the inhabitants of the Netherlands East Indies, 90 per cent of those in British India, and lesser proportions in other lands.

In short, the work hitherto done by Christian missionary agencies should now become the concern of governments working through international organizations on a worldwide scale. The time has come for the flag and the cross to face the same task. If the United States and Great Britain show themselves truly Christian nations in the relief and rehabilitation programs and at the peace table, they will demonstrate to the Oriental millions that Christianity is something to be desired, and the doors of the world will be opened for a spiritual advance such as was never dreamed in the days before the war. But if victors fail to reveal the Christlike spirit now, God help us!

Yet in the face of this unprecedented opportunity many voices are raised to ridicule the proposal of freedom from want, not only as impossible, but as improvident. Granted that men could be freed from actual want, would that freedom lull them into laziness? It would be ruinous to lose the personal virtues of industry, prudence, thrift. These are integral to Christian culture. Can a social system of insurance against want be devised which will not destroy individual initiative and enterprise?

Sir William Beveridge proposes a plan of compulsory insurance against sickness, old age, and unemployment. Under his plan the individual would be forced to save for his old age, for his wife's maternity benefits, for his children's schooling, for his periods of sickness and unemployment. The Emersonian principle of self-help in Beveridge's plan removes the stigma of charity from it and does not encourage anyone in the belief that the government owes him a living. "There is no danger of creating a nation of people that will not want to work. In any case, they would not have the chance, because the unemployment benefit, which, incidentally, is only a small part of the whole scheme, is administered through what we call employment exchanges. The man goes there and if a job is offered to him he cannot refuse that job and still get his benefit unless he can prove he was reasonable in refusing." [3]

Of course no system of social insurance can be made proof against the shirker. Here, as elsewhere, success depends on the spirit in which the program is worked; and every new social advance makes more imperative the union of Paul's two counsels to the Galatians: "Bear ye one another's burdens," and, "Every man shall bear his own burden." The aim of Christian culture is to create dependables, not dependents.

While we seek to safeguard freedom from want against

[3] Sir William Beveridge, in *Talks,* Columbia Broadcasting System, Inc., Vol. VIII, No. 3, 1943.

deteriorating into freedom from work, we must remember how much the sense of economic security can be a spur to creative effort. Think how blighting is the shadow of an insecure old age. Think how the faculties of an unmarried business woman are depressed if she is constantly faced with the prospect of an uncared for future. Think how initiative of effort can be killed when tomorrow and tomorrow stretches out in a vision of unending drudgery. While it is true that hunger is a goad, it is also true that there is a point beyond which hunger depresses rather than drives. The specter of starvation may serve as a scarecrow to frighten the lazy, but it does not prove an inspiration to higher mental effort. Necessity is the mother of invention, but our most prized inventions were not mothered by persons who lacked the necessities of life. "The United States was not discovered by men who were hungry."

FREEDOM FROM FEAR

Logically the fourth of the famous freedoms should be listed first. Unless we can free ourselves from fear, there can be no genuine freedom of speech or worship, no real freedom from want.

And the prescription for this freedom as formulated in the presidental pronouncement is so partial that it barely touches the fringes of the full issues involved: "Freedom from fear, which translated into world terms means a world-wide reduction of armaments to such a point that no nation will be in a position to commit an act of physical aggression against any neighbor." Such is the officially suggested cure for the fear which now bedevils the sons of men. Essential and desirable as is the reduction of the back-breaking armaments which beget fear and breed war, realism requires that we

recognize how distant is such a goal from our present mood
and also how far short of banishing fear world-wide disarmament would fall.

Granted that we can pull the teeth of aggressor nations in a
way to prevent their attacks, men would still be fearful of
economic insecurities. And if we could make the world
wantproof as well as warproof, we should still run the risks
of disease and accident. And if health programs and safety
campaigns reduced these dangers to a minimum, the best
of bodily machines would still run down, and eventually
we would confront

> the dread of something after death,
> The undiscovered country from whose bourn
> No traveler returns.

If we are to attain freedom from fear, we must envisage the
full range of human experience. Fear is a realm which can
be conquered only by gaining control of the air, the atmosphere, in which "we live, and move, and have our being."

There was nothing which Christ felt called upon to challenge more frequently than fear. As a friend he saw that fear
hounded his friends from birth to death and drove them into
all sorts of pitfalls. As a teacher he discovered how fear
blinded the minds of men, making them unwilling to face
facts or to trust themselves to truth. As a physician Jesus
found that fear paralyzed men's faculties, poisoned their
emotions, and sapped their energies. He would never have
earned the title of Master had he not been able to control
fear, both his own and that of others.

The spirit of Christ spreads a contagion of healthy-mindedness which dissolves many fears. Some persons have a way
of setting the nerves of those around them on edge, starting

mutual distrusts, stirring suspicions and animosities. Others radiate calmness, confidence, courage. A school superintendent, discussing the teachers who had served in his system, pointed out that professional training and academic degrees do not guarantee ability to maintain discipline. Some teachers seem to generate disorder, others to beget a spirit which brings out the best in those around them.

Christ stirs up the gift of God which is in us, that native wholesomeness of mind which is a part of the childlike spirit essential to entrance into the kingdom of heaven. "For God hath not given us the spirit of fear; but of power, and of love, and of a sound mind." Christ restores that healthy spirit which cures us of both wishful thinking and wasteful anxiety by reminding us that "if hopes were dupes, fears may be liars." He dispels the mirage of fear, which is just as bedeviling a reality as the mirage of hope. Into a world where men are living on the defensive, sunk in their suspicions, Christ comes with the heartening and healing power of a physician entering a sickroom. His invigorating faith in human nature lifts men out of their low distrusts. His high-mindedness shames men out of their petty suspicions.

The Christ spirit imparts a clarity of vision along with healthiness of mind. The first step in the conquest of fear is a knowledge of its source and nature. That is the principle on which the psychologist works. Christ bids us probe to the roots of our fears. But he also would have us do what Thomas Carlyle did when, after a period of sleeplessness and despair, he forced himself to face the worst that life might inflict upon him and to ask whether he could not endure it. Carlyle finally decided that in no event would he go through life whimpering like a coward, that whatever came he could meet and defy it. When we thus beset our fears behind and before, we checkmate them with understanding and courage.

Furthermore, Christ sets our fears in a long perspective which levels out the hills of difficulty. When he bade us "be not anxious for the morrow," he was counseling not the closed eye but the long view, which looks beyond the to-morrows. A more spacious historic sense does much to de-liver us from some despairs. Do we think that human nature is becoming more cruel because the twentieth century has shed more blood than its predecessors? Then let us remember that in the nineteenth century little children were hitched to coal cars in the mines. Cruelty, like other things, may be better organized today; but the spirit of man is becoming more humane. In 1840 Britain made war on China to force the admission of opium. There was then no outcry of an outraged world, but the world's conscience would cry out today. In 1854 the American ministers to England, France, and Spain met at Ostend and signed a manifesto urging the United States to make war on Spain and take Cuba from her by force if Spain should refuse to sell that island to us for slavery purposes. Viewed against such a background, even the current atrocity stories cannot blur the fact that the human conscience is growing more sensitive.

Moreover, the Christ spirit begets an invulnerability which makes us immune to some fears. When our concern is pri-marily for character, we are sheathed against irritating at-tacks on our reputation. When we rid ourselves of pride and conceit, we are not tortured by the curse of social comparisons. When we want money only for use and not for power, the torment of financial worries largely disappears. Few of us are fearful of lacking what Christ called the necessities of life. One factor in freeing us from want is freeing us from wanting.

And most important of all, the spirit of Christ points toward that "perfect love" which "casteth out fear." It may seem sheer sentimentality to toss that scriptural statement into the midst of our global gladiators. We know that "perfect love casteth out fear" and distrust from the bosom of a family. But when we speak of "the family of nations," the phrase is an empty euphemism.

Yet while love seems temporarily helpless in the face of Hitlers and Tojos, perhaps there is an angle from which we Americans can use brotherly love to banish fear. When we talk about freedom from fear, we have in mind our fear of others. But how about the fear others have of us? In Mexico and Latin America there is much apprehension concerning the great "Colossus of the North." And one reason that the Germans will remain loyal to Hitler in their losing fight after hope is dead is that we, along with others, twenty-five years ago helped to kill by starvation their hope of better treatment at the hands of their conquerors. Behind our terms of "unconditional surrender" the Germans behold the specter of that former blockade from whose victims Hitler recruited his followers. When the guns cease this time, shall we show a spirit brotherly enough to cast out fear from the youth who are making Europe's tomorrow? And before firing stops we can cultivate a good will sufficient to still the fears of our neighbors to the south; of the Chinese, whom we have been wounding by our Exclusion Act; of the Russians, for whom our admiration is alloyed with so much suspicion; yes, even of the Japanese within our borders, whom we have interned.

The statesman must henceforth stand beside the missionary. Mental disarmament must advance alongside military disarmament—or a little ahead. Instead of the cross's following the flag in the wake of imperial expansion, the flags of the strong nations must follow the cross in the service of the Son of Man who "came not to be ministered unto, but to minister."

Yet despite all social safeguards the spirit of man is not free from fear until he feels at home in a universe which he can trust. Here is voiced the full attainment of this fourth freedom: "I am persuaded, that neither death, nor life, nor angels, nor principalities, nor powers, nor things present, nor things to come, nor height, nor depth, nor any other creature, shall be able to separate us from the love of God, which is in Christ Jesus our Lord." [4] Such is the faith which insures the "blessings of liberty."

[4] Rom. 8:38-39.

to ourselves and our Posterity

The vitality of a culture or civilization is tested by the care of its young. A society is degenerate and done for when it lives only for the present, saying with the profligate Louis XV of France: "After us, the deluge." The virility of our American way of life has been attested hitherto by the oft-quoted statement that education is the American passion.

In one of his last speeches Woodrow Wilson said: "My clients are the children. My clients are the next generation. They do not know what promises and bonds I undertook when I ordered the armies of the United States to the soil of France, but I know, and I intend to redeem my pledges to the children. They shall not be sent upon a similar errand." [1]

Woodrow Wilson's pledge to the children of his day was not redeemed. Many of the lads whose faces were lighted by the hopes of 1919 have perished in Guadalcanal and Tunisia. And some there are who now say that two world wars within the space of a single generation point to the "decline and fall of Western culture." Are we caught in a vicious circle of inevitably recurring wars which mean that our modern machine civilization has reached a dead end?

We refuse to surrender to such pessimism. We were nourished on the American dream—the dream of a land where life shall be richer and better, with opportunity for every per-

[1] As quoted in *New York Times,* November 6, 1943.

152

son according to his ability and achievement. That dream is perhaps America's greatest contribution to the world. And we are determined that it shall not die in our hands.

But if the blessings of liberty are to be secured "to ourselves and our posterity," we must make youth not only our clients but our partners. In pleading for national unity in America, let us foster a league of ages. Think what partnership between younger and older minds does. It makes the home not a paternalism of parents nor a bolshevism of youth but a partnership of free minds wherein the experiences of the elder supplement and guide the experiments of the younger. It helps the oldsters who have become jaded by compromise to look into the fresh, unflinching faith of the young. It helps the old in renewing their enthusiasms and the young in ripening their expectations. It joins the treasures of memory and experience with the riches of hope and confidence. We would stop so many of these recurring social iniquities if we could retain the idealism of the early twenties until we come into the power and prestige of the late forties and fifties. But the parabolic course of our ideals is so tragically like that of the doctor in Cronin's *The Citadel*. After he had yielded to the seductions of success, his young wife attempted to recall him to his earlier idealism. "Don't you remember," she asked, "how you used to speak of life, that it was an attack on the unknown, an assault uphill—as though you had to take some castle that you knew was there, but couldn't see, on the top?" With a shrug of his shoulders, the doctor answered, "Oh! I was young then—foolish. That was just romantic talk." [2]

Governmentally speaking, America is no longer one of the younger members in the family of nations. In the quartet of

[2] Little, Brown & Co., 1937, pp. 299-300.

United Nations which will play a major part in shaping the
world of tomorrow Great Britain, our mother country, is of
course much older; but China is still in the growing pains
of national organization, and Russia is a lusty youth of
twenty-five years. If we are to carry our end of the reconstruction work, we must demonstrate a vitality comparable to that
of Russia. Only a dynamic democracy can be safely teamed
with a self-confident communistic state.

Gilbert Murray tells us that the world at the time of Jesus'
birth was suffering from failure of nerve. The ideals of divine fatherhood and human brotherhood were present. The
Stoics believed in human freedom and denounced slavery as
unnatural. But, like their eminent spokesman Marcus Aure-
lius, they viewed the poor and oppressed as from a lofty
mountain top. They saw the inequities that beset men, but
they lacked the nerve to challenge them. When Jesus came,
he identified himself with the hungry, the weak, the im-
prisoned, the downtrodden. And to "as many as received him,
to them gave he power to become the sons of God." Thus
he quickened the failing nerves and thereby started reforms
which eventually wiped out slavery, alleviated poverty, and
sowed the seeds of democracy.

We must recover from any lack of faith or failure of
nerve in our democratic way of life. The basic ideals and institutions of our land were born in the heart of a young and
vigorous people. Recent events only serve to reveal the
soundness of the foundations laid by our national founders.
When the little "Mayflower" lay off Plymouth Rock after
the hazardous voyage, the Pilgrims drew up the Mayflower
Compact, declaring that the trip had been undertaken " for
yᵉ glorie of God, and advancemente of yᵉ Christian faith, and
honour of our king & country." Suppose that, instead of such

a fundamental religious faith, the Pilgrims had merely held the Nazi belief in a superior race destined to rule by force. With such a creed they might have driven out the Indians, but they could not have created the Commonwealth of Massachusetts. With a philosophy of racial superiority and ruthless force men can destroy existing cultures, but they cannot build and perpetuate lasting societies.

With their religious faith and philosophy our Founding Fathers developed a dignity of life, even in the midst of crude physical environment. Consider the simple, pure lines of the early New England meeting houses. Or contrast Boston's "Sons of Liberty" with Hitler's Storm Troopers. Under Sam Adams the former made Boston a rather turbulent place with their "Tea Party" and other rough tactics. But they never manifested the modern Nazi spirit of brutality. When the American patriots were out at Bunker Hill fighting the British, many of them had left their wives and children in Boston. Yet General Gage and his British troops did not mistreat those families. Nor did the Colonial troops take cruel revenge on the Tory sympathizers when they regained Boston. Ours has been a heritage of humaneness and dignity despite lawless frontiers, business buccaneering, and rough conditions of living. Individual life has had more value along the Hudson and the Mississippi than along the Yangtze and the Ganges—a fact which we should remember when we become impatient with China's struggle for national untity and Britain's slowness in developing self-government within India. Democracy can flourish only on a soil fertilized by faith in the worth and dignity of the individual.

As custodian of this religious and civic heritage we must cultivate not only enduring values but coming values. We must live on the growing edge of things. God hath chosen

"things which are not, to bring to nought things that are."
Our faith must be sufficiently creative to see the tree in the
apple, to catch the scent of spring in the winds of winter, to
taste "the powers of the world to come." To live for values
still in the bud, to live for something so big that it goes on
when our physical strength flags with age, to prefer personal
failure in a cause that will triumph rather than a personal
success in a movement eventually to fail—such is our role if
we are to fulfill Burke's conception of society as a compact
between the living, the dead, and the yet unborn.

The streets of Old Boston or of Greenwich Village in New
York are quaint and interesting. Laid on the lines of least
resistance, they were quite adequate for the traffic of those
early settlements. The day came, however, when New York
awoke to the fact that she was destined to be a great city.
Then she projected her streets and avenues with that straight-
ness which is so well known to every resident. And when the
motor era grew apace, New York built those magnificent
parkways which have replaced the winding roads of West-
chester and New Jersey. As with a city, so it is with a national society. We cannot carry the traffic of a new day in
the crooked lanes of an old order. If we are to keep our date
with destiny, we must cut through the meshwork of expediency with the straight lines of principle; we must make
both straight and wide the highway of God in the wilderness
of men.

That we are not facing a dead end, but rather a challenging task of spiritual and social engineering is the faith which
must now firmly grip us. Justice Wiley Rutledge has pointed
out that we need this faith and hope even more than we
need improved legal instruments. The first problem "is rather
one of creating or re-creating in the national heart a hope to

replace its present despair, a confidence to overcome its doubt. That is a problem of the statesman-priest, for the grace of statesmen is the grace of priests to his people. He approaches divinity in his power to bring hope from despair, confidence from doubt, assurance from uncertainty, in short, the sense that life is worth living and fighting to live.

"People need this more than they need democracy as we have known it or any other nation has known it. They need an ideal, a goal, a direction, which colors all their thought and feeling—subconsciously, perhaps, but surely. If they have this, and believe it or some of it can be achieved, they can survive any temporary tyranny. The task is essentially religious."[3]

In Ponca City, Oklahoma, is symbolized the figure of "The Pioneer Woman;" the statue represents a woman, her face up, her eyes alight, with a Bible under her right arm, her left hand holding the hand of a young lad with whom she is stepping briskly forward. The pioneer women of our land took the Bible as the book of life, transmitted it through their bodies and blood, and then passed its principles on to their children, with whom they kept in step, walking bravely and hopefully forward to a better day. Such was the spirit which made America, and such only is the spirit which can save her future.

[3] Wiley Rutledge, in *Science, Philosophy and Religion,* Second Symposium, p. 189.